W9-BMD-304

Service-Learning and Social Justice

Engaging Students in Social Change

Susan Benigni Cipolle

ROWMAN & LITTLEFIELD PUBLISHERS, INC.
Lanham • New York • Toronto • Plymouth, UK

Rowman & Littlefield, Inc.
A wholly owned subsidary of The Rowman & Littlefield Publishing Group, Inc.
4501 Forbes Boulevard, Suite 200, Lanham, Maryland 20706
http://www.rowmanlittlefield.com

Estover Road, Plymouth PL6 7PY, United Kingdom

British Library Cataloguing in Publication Information Available

Library of Congress Cataloging-in-Publication Data

Cipolle, Susan Benigni, 1953-
 Service-learning and social justice : engaging students in social change / Susan Benigni Cipolle.
 p. cm.
 Includes bibliographical references.
 ISBN 978-1-60709-518-7 (cloth : alk. paper) — ISBN 978-1-60709-519-4 (pbk. : alk. paper) — ISBN 978-1-60709-520-0 (electronic)
 1. Service-learning—United States. 2. Social justice—Study and teaching—United States. I. Title.
 LC221.C535 2010
 361.3'7—dc22   2009043123

⊗ ™ The paper used in this publication meets the minimum requirements of American National Standard for Information Sciences—Permanence of Paper for Printed Library Materials, ANSI/NISO Z39.48-1992.

Printed in the United States of America

I dedicate this book to all teachers who regard education as an act of social justice and to my students—past, present, and future—who inspire me in my efforts and give me confidence in the future.

Contents

Preface

Service-learning at its best: "Life isn't fair, and people don't always get what they deserve. How far are we going to let people fall before we say this is not acceptable?"

Service-learning at its worst: "I don't understand. If unemployment is so high on the reservation, how come we are painting their houses?"

These quotes, and others like them, were the catalyst for my investigation into the upside and downside of service-learning and the source of my inspiration and motivation to write this book.

My Journey

I began my education career as a French teacher at Benilde—St. Margaret's School (BSM) in 1976 and saw both my children graduate from there. Currently, in addition to teaching, I am assistant to the president. I have witnessed firsthand, from many perspectives, the tremendous positive influence that service-learning has on students, schools, and the communities in which we work. Over the last thirty years, my philosophy of education and my vocation as a teacher have evolved as I came to a realization: I am not teaching French; I'm teaching kids. My path changed as I learned about and embraced multicultural education, service-learning, Catholic social teachings, and critical pedagogy. Through these four interwoven threads, I gained new insights and a more complex understanding of education and the dynamics of service.

I was convinced that connecting multicultural education and service-learning was necessary for empowering students to better understand the world and have a positive impact on society. Multicultural education draws attention to inequity and injustice in our world, which can leave students feeling guilty, overwhelmed, or powerless. Service-learning is the action component for those feelings, providing opportunities to fight injustice.

In my experience, multicultural education highlights social problems (who, what, where), service-learning shows how we can make change, and *Catholic social teachings* convey why action is crucial. Catholic social teachings identify seven familiar principles that serve as a guide for living, providing a framework for integrating values throughout the curriculum and answering the question, what are we called to do? The principles are life and dignity of the human person, call to family, community and participation, rights and responsibilities, options for the poor and vulnerable, the dignity of work and the rights of workers, solidarity, and care for the earth.

Recognizing that these values are not uniquely Catholic, other faith-based schools and secular institutions can find similar guidelines for morality and ethics in character education programs, the basic tenets of humanism,[1] or documents such as the United States Declaration of Independence, the United Nations' Universal Declaration of Human Rights, and the United Nations Convention on the Rights of the Child. The Preamble of the Universal Declaration of Human Rights, which is the foundation of freedom, justice, and peace in the world, affirms the inherent dignity and equal and inalienable rights of the human family. This document details thirty human rights including freedom, equal treatment despite differences, freedom of speech, freedom of religion and association, and the right to work, leisure time, and education.

In 2002, I entered the critical pedagogy doctoral program at the University of St. Thomas in Minneapolis, beginning my study with Paulo Freire's *Pedagogy of the Oppressed*, Ira Shor's *Empowering Education*, and bell hooks's *Teaching to Transgress*. I was convinced that service-learning was a prime example of a counterhegemonic educational practice that results in transformative social action. However, I was provoked to examine the topic more critically.

Upon completing a three-day seminar with Shor, I asked if he thought service-learning was an application of critical pedagogy, to which he replied, "It can be." This simple statement led me into four years of study and research on the strengths and limitations of service-learning and how individuals develop a *social-justice* orientation to service. As I came to view service-learning through a *critical* lens, examining issues of power, privilege, and oppression, I began to see a downside of service learning underneath the gleaming surface of good will.

Background of the Study

One of the primary missions of education is to prepare students for democratic and civic engagement. I believe as educators it is our responsibility to help students acquire the necessary information, skills, and desire to be engaged citizens who can meet not only today's social and economic challenges but who will also work to eradicate the root causes of inequity and injustice. Service-learning, which is widely used in public and private K–16 education, has the potential to build skills, attitudes, and behaviors connecting students to their community, as well as creating a lifelong pattern of active citizenship.

The litany of positive service-learning outcomes is widely recognized. Research studies show that students involved in service-learning demonstrate academic and personal growth in such areas as empowerment, leadership, and character development.[2] Researchers also demonstrate how service-learning can positively impact society not only through the work of students today, but also by increasing their connection to community, promoting racial understanding, and cultivating a dedication to future service for social justice.[3]

University multicultural education courses—and particularly teacher-education programs—use service-learning to help students develop a broader perspective on, and critical awareness of, reality and other peoples' experiences.[4] As the percentage of students of color continues to increase in many school districts across the nation, teacher education programs seek to better prepare the predominantly White, female pool of candidates for changing demographics through service experiences in diverse communities. However, research results show limited success.

It is difficult to get preservice teachers to see marginalized communities in the context of larger power struggles, and some White, preservice teachers see themselves as "saviors," maintaining a deficit view of the children they are tutoring.[5] Students' essays often reflect minimal growth toward a critical understanding of reality,[6] and they have difficulty critically reflecting on both their personal biases and the structural causes of poverty at the same time.[7]

While there is unlimited potential for service-learning to promote praxis for social change, variation in the underlying ideologies and implementation of service programs can mediate positive outcomes.[8] Some program characteristics and orientations reinforce stereotypes, exploit the population being served, and result in maintaining the status quo of inequity and injustice.[9] Recognizing the complexity of service-learning experiences, many researchers report that the effects are dependent on many issues, including type of service, quality of placement, quality of teacher and course reflection, and the duration and intensity of work.[10]

Having a critical understanding of the strengths and limitations of service-learning and seeing many BSM alumni who were living lives committed to social justice convinced me to investigate the link between service and social justice.

The Study

My original research examined the relationship between school-age service experiences and adult behavior and attitudes toward service and social justice. I was also interested in developing a theory on how individuals become committed to social justice. Because we had been offering service classes at BSM for over a quarter of a century, I drew study participants from BSM alumni from 1975 to 1999. This provided a sampling of adults who could reflect on the effect of their high-school service experience at a distance of five to twenty-five years.

There were two phases to my research. First, I sent questionnaires to randomly selected graduates and analyzed the survey data to examine a range of experiences and attitudes about service from a broad base of individuals. Then I conducted in-depth interviews with eleven alumni who were actively working for social justice. I wanted to understand their beliefs and orientation to service, the influences and factors that led them to advocate for social justice, and how they perceived the outcomes and consequences of their social-justice work.

The analysis of the data collected from questionnaires and interviews resulted in a three-part theory on how individuals develop a social-justice orientation to service-learning. This theory presents four essential elements that lead to *critical-consciousness* development; three stages of White critical-conscious development; and stage-appropriate information, experiences, and reflection to increase students' critical consciousness.[11]

This Book

This book shares my experience, research findings, and conclusions on service-learning and social justice in an accessible, straightforward manner that is useful to elementary and secondary teachers, administrators, university professors, and preservice teachers. As a high-school classroom teacher and administrator, a recent doctoral student, and an adjunct college professor,

I draw on my varied experience to offer a framework including *theory* (how things work) and *practice* (what you can do) to build a service-learning program that fosters students' critical consciousness and their commitment to engage in social change. I hope you find this thought provoking and helpful. The French teacher in me says "*Bon Courage!*"; and, as my dad always used to say, "*Sempre Avanti!*"

Acknowledgments

This book is the outcome of a personal and professional journey that began with my work in multicultural education and then encompassed service-learning, Catholic social teachings, and critical pedagogy. I am indebted to the many individuals who shared their gifts as they traveled with me along the path as well as to those who made my journey possible.

I am grateful to the community of Benilde–St. Margaret's School for fostering an environment that values lifelong learning and supports individuals in their pursuit of knowledge. I want express my appreciation to school leaders Jim Hamburge, Bob Tift, Stacy Furness, and Sue Skinner, as well as to my service-learning colleagues and friends Connie Fourré, Lisa Lenhart-Murphy, Holly Hoey Germann, and Zach Zeckser. I also need to recognize and thank my good friend Mary Periolat, who pioneered diversity and multicultural initiatives at Benilde–St. Margaret's.

In addition, I am grateful to Sister Marie Herbert Seiter, CSJ, and the Sisters of St. Joseph of Carondelet for supporting me and my research. Their long history of commitment to social justice and praxis is inspirational. I appreciate the excellent faculty at the University of St. Thomas, in particular those who reviewed my research—Dr. Karen Westberg, Dr. Eleni Roulis, and Dr. Jan Hansen—and the Murray Institute, for giving me the opportunity to teach Cohorts XV and XVII.

This book would not have been possible without the participation of the graduates from Benilde–St. Margaret's classes of 1975–1999. I also acknowledge Patrice Carlson, Paula Leider, and Karen McCauley for their help in moving from data, to dissertation, to completed manuscript, as well as Patti Belcher, acquisition editor at Rowman & Littlefield. I am also indebted to Ira Shor, Carolyn O'Grady, and Stephen Brookfield, who generously agreed to read the manuscript and endorse its publication.

Finally, I want to acknowledge and thank my family. I am grateful to my husband, Bob, our children, Christina and Tony, and my Uncle Joe Benigni for their unconditional love, inspiration, and encouragement.

PART I

UNDERSTANDING THE SOCIAL-JUSTICE MODEL FOR SERVICE-LEARNING

CHAPTER ONE

Overview of the Social-Justice Model for Service-Learning

I have often wondered why authors make readers wait until the conclusion to know "the answer." This chapter presents the whole picture regarding how you can build a service-learning program fostering student action for social change. I offer an introduction to the four essential elements of critical consciousness, the three stages of critical-consciousness development, and tools you can use to support students as they embark on this journey.

But first, as a language teacher, I believe we need to bring clarity to some terms and concepts. In everyday life, people use expressions that they understand in general but have a difficult time articulating. Additionally, the educational community often takes fuzziness to a whole new level. For instance, in my critical-pedagogy doctoral cohort, twenty-five intelligent people struggled for four years to clearly and concisely define *critical pedagogy*; and, for years, I sought definitions of *social justice* and *critical consciousness* and even tried Googling the terms without receiving meaningful results.

Part of the reason we struggle to define such terms is that concepts can have different meanings to different people in different contexts. Additionally, words, whether intentionally or not, often become co-opted and infused with coded implications and political overtones. For example, some people are uncomfortable using the term *social justice*, because others may see it as either a religious term or a political agenda. But isn't "social justice" synonymous with transformative social action, civic engagement for equity, or moral and civic responsibility? These terms seem more acceptable to a wider audience.

In that spirit, let's clarify several concepts, so we are starting at the same place and can progress from there. Additional terms are defined as they occur throughout the book, as well as collected in a glossary in the appendices.

Key Concept Areas

As an introduction to these definitions, we must first examine the term *critical*. This word has many meanings. People often think of being "critical" as disapproving and negative, while others use *critical* to mean "vital or important." In still other instances, *critical* can mean "dangerous or life threatening." In my writings, I draw upon Stephen Brookfield's definition, which insists that for something to be *critical*—whether in critical learning, critical analysis, critical reflection, or critical pedagogy—individuals must examine power relations inherent in the situation or context; question the underlying assumptions on race, gender, and class; and understand its connection to the dominant ideology.[1]

Community Service, Service-Learning, and Critical Service-Learning

There are so many definitions of *service-learning* that when I first started my work, I needed to construct a definition I could use to clearly and concisely explain it to others:

> Service-learning is a learning strategy in which students have leadership roles in thoughtfully organized service experiences that meet real needs in the community. The service is integrated into the students' academic studies with structured time to research, reflect, discuss, and connect their experiences to their learning and their worldview.[2]

Explaining the difference between *community service* and service-learning can be difficult. I find the following example composed by the National Youth Leadership Council helpful:

- Cleaning up a riverbank is SERVICE.
- Sitting in a science classroom looking at water samples under a microscope is LEARNING.
- Science students taking samples from local water sources, then analyzing the samples, documenting the results and presenting the scientific information to a pollution control agency is SERVICE-LEARNING.[3]

Critical service-learning is a distinct subset of service-learning. While there are many worthwhile service projects that meet real needs in the community, for service-learning to be critical, students and teachers need to examine issues of power, privilege, and oppression; question the hidden bias and assumptions of race, class, and gender; and work to change the social and economic system for equity and justice. To include *activism* in the previous example, we add a fourth dimension:

- Science students creating public service announcements to raise awareness of human impact on water quality in order to change community attitudes and behavior is CRITICAL SERVICE-LEARNING.

Multicultural Education, Critical Multiculturalism, and Critical Pedagogy

Multicultural education is another term with many construed meanings, ranging from celebrating cultures and customs, to diversity training for tolerance or acceptance of others, to examining agents and targets of oppression. Analyzing issues from different perspectives is often included as a component of multicultural education. Here is a brief summary of several leading educators' views on multicultural education.

According to James Bank, *multiculturalism* is an idea that there should be educational equity for all students; educational reform to ensure that all students have an equal chance for success; and a process of striving for the goals of equality and eliminating discrimination. To that end, *multicultural education* should be broadly defined to include content integration, the knowledge-construction process, prejudice reduction, equity pedagogy, and the empowering of the school culture and social structure.[4]

Sonia Nieto's definition in *Affirming Diversity* incorporates a wide-angle view of multicultural education by highlighting that it is antiracist, basic, important for all students, pervasive, socially just, process oriented, and critical:

> Multicultural education is a process of comprehensive school reform and basic education for all students. It challenges and rejects racism and other forms of discrimination in schools and society and accepts and affirms pluralism (ethnic, racial, linguistic, religious, economic, and gender among others) that students, their communities and teachers reflect. Multicultural education permeates the schools' curriculum and instructional strategies as well as the interactions among teachers, students, and families . . . Because it uses critical pedagogy as its underlying philosophy and focuses on knowledge, reflection,

and action (praxis) as the basis for social change, multicultural education promotes democratic principles of social justice.[5]

For a comprehensive explanation of variations in multiculturalism, I suggest Joe Kincheloe and Shirley R. Steinberg's book *Changing Multiculturalism*.[6] They provide a detailed description of five stances of multicultural education: conservative/monoculturalism, liberal multiculturalism, pluralist multiculturalism, left-essentialist multiculturalism, and *critical multiculturalism*. In a similar manner, Carl Grant and Christine Sleeter organize five approaches to multicultural education as follows: exceptional and culturally different, human relations, single-group, mainstream multicultural education, and critical multiculturalism.[7]

As a classroom teacher, my working definition for *multicultural education* evolved over time, but one metaphor has remained constant: multicultural education is like the proverbial three-legged stool. It must impact the content you teach; the student-centered teaching and learning strategies you use; and the climate, relationships, and policies you create in the classroom and school community.

Additionally, I have learned that multicultural education goes beyond learning about others, most emphatically beginning with learning about yourself. It requires looking at your beliefs, attitudes, biases, and assumptions; assessing their origins; and reevaluating who benefits from the existing social system and who is disadvantaged. "Studying 'the other,'" state bell hooks and Cornel West, "is not the goal, the goal is learning about some aspect of who you are."[8]

Critical multiculturalism, also called "social reconstructionist multicultural education," is transformative because its goal is achieving awareness of the social, economic, and political forces shaping society in order to change society. This requires questioning our formerly unexamined beliefs and assumptions, thinking critically about reality, and challenging the policies and practices that reproduce inequality and injustice.[9]

While there are many approaches to critical pedagogy in the classroom, its fundamental goal is to examine the educational system critically and work to transform the dominant social and cultural values in the interest of a more equitable democracy.[10] My short version is that critical pedagogy empowers students to change the world, creating the ability to see reality as it is and critically ask "Why?" Students are active participants in creating knowledge through critical inquiry, reflection, and action. Classroom strategies and activities include problem posing; research and analysis of issues examining power and oppression; and questioning one's assumptions, beliefs, and perceptions.[11]

Critical service-learning, critical multiculturalism, and critical pedagogy intersect with the same underlying goal of social transformation. They also incorporate similar teaching strategies of critical analysis, reflection, and action. Differences lie in their originating movements: service-learning is rooted in experiential education, multicultural education grew out of the civil rights movement of the 1960s, and critical pedagogy is grounded in Paulo Freire's work for adult literacy and liberation in Brazil in the 1970s.

Critical Consciousness, Social Justice, Praxis, and Phronesis

The path to social change begins with developing a critical consciousness. In general, this means having an accurate view of reality, but we can benefit from a less ambiguous description. The four elements of critical consciousness development are

- developing a deeper awareness of self
- developing a deeper awareness and broader perspective of others
- developing a deeper awareness and broader perspective of social issues
- seeing one's potential to make change[12]

The most functional definition of *social justice* I have found is in *Educating Citizens: Preparing America's Undergraduates for Lives of Moral and Civic Responsibility*, edited by Anne Colby and others. They define social justice education as a contribution "to social change and public policies that increase gender and racial equality, end discrimination of various kinds, and reduce the stark income inequalities that characterize this country and most of the world."[13]

Critical educators often discuss the importance of *praxis*, which is critical reflection and action with the goal of social change for equity and justice. Peter McLaren adds another dimension by arguing that "praxis (informed actions) must be guided by phronesis (the disposition to act truly and rightly) . . . [meaning] actions and knowledge must be directed at eliminating pain, oppression, and inequality, and at promoting justice and freedom."[14]

With a working understanding of these key concepts, teachers who want to create effective service-learning programs must focus on being critical. It is important to examine power relations and question assumptions about yourself, your philosophy of education, and your curricula. In becoming a critical multiculturalist, dedicated to social change, you can inspire your students to work for social justice as you guide them on their journey to a critical consciousness.

Education as an Act of Social Justice

It is a common thought that teaching is only about the transmission of knowledge and usable skills: education should be apolitical, and teachers should not have a particular agenda. At first glance, this makes sense. However, in reality everything we do in school has political implications, from the choice and delivery of curriculum, to the policies regarding discipline, testing, tracking, funding, and ultimately who has access to power within the school community. We have only to look at students' experiences and achievement within and among schools to recognize the extent of disparity and injustice. Schools can serve to support the status quo by privileging students from dominant groups, or they can be sites of change by empowering students to be active, critical citizens who will question and transform society.

Education becomes an act of social justice when seen as part of a larger democratic process dedicated to equality and equity in schools and in society. Teachers seek to connect the curriculum to students' lives and the world around them and guide students in critical inquiry, reflection, and action so they can identify and solve problems. Based on the democratic values of freedom, justice, and equality, teaching results in questioning the status quo and becomes an act of resistance against injustices.[15]

To effectively provide this type of learning environment, we must first examine the purpose of education and understand our role as educators. The term *education* comes from the Latin *educare*, meaning "to bring up or rear." It is related to *educere*, meaning "to lead out."[16] Thomas Groome, in *Educating for Life*, notes that "Plato described teaching as 'turning the soul' of learners and he meant touching and shaping the innermost 'being'—their identity and agency."[17] Clearly, the purpose of education is broader than simply providing content and skills. This belief is grounded in the philosophy that our children should not only be knowledgeable, talented, and skilled, they should be moral and ethical contributors to the community.

As teachers interested in equity and justice, we bring who we are and what we believe to the classroom. We need to be aware and critically reflect on our beliefs and motivations. In order to articulate this, we must recognize the relationship between our educational philosophy and our political views.

With this in mind, let's examine the term *agenda*. There is a fine line—a small semantic difference—between *having* an agenda and *pushing* an agenda. How our agenda is perceived is determined by how we express our motivation. Do we ground it in educational philosophy or a political ideology? An educational agenda incorporates the school's mission, teachers' philosophy of education, and beliefs about students. When an agenda is seen as biased or political, it can be perceived as something manipulative or narrow in scope and can undermine the broader purpose of education.

Obviously, there is an overlap between our personal political views and our philosophy of education. And yet, in a democratic classroom, students must be at the center of the educational experience, creating their own ideas, beliefs, and view of the world. Teachers who regard education as an act of social justice need to have a profound respect for and confidence in students. Our role is to support students and create learning experiences where they gain factual information, critically reflect, and grapple with reality.

Road Map to Social Change through Service-Learning

The social-justice model for service-learning has three core components. Figure 1.1 depicts the road map through these core components: the four essential elements of critical consciousness, the three stages of White[18] critical-consciousness development, and the strategies for navigating them. This theory, developed from interviews and survey responses from Benilde–St. Margaret's School (BSM) alumni, provides a framework for educators dedicated to education for social change.

Four Essential Elements of Critical Consciousness

As I spoke to individuals committed to social justice, I heard about their families, early service experiences, and high-school, college, and adult experiences and attitudes regarding service and social justice. In synthesizing their common experiences, attitudes, and beliefs, it became clear that they serve as building blocks for developing a critical consciousness and a social-justice orientation to service. Furthermore, these collective early experiences contribute to developing a deeper self-awareness, a deeper awareness and broader perspective of others and of social issues, and the potential to create change.

Achieving a deeper self-awareness means having a clear understanding of your level of privilege, your values, your role in society, and your responsibility to others. Participation in service and discussions about moral and civic obligations help individuals clarify their values and become committed to work for the common good. Young people, working alongside adults, confronting issues of poverty and discrimination, see social-justice work as a possibility for themselves. It provides a basis for them to see their own privilege

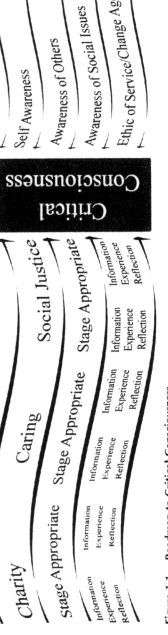

Figure 1.1. Roadmap to Critical Consciousness

Figure 1.2. Four Essential Elements of Critical Consciousness Development

and power and examine how their actions can contribute to or fight against the status quo.

For White, middle-class students, gaining a deeper awareness and broader perspective of others often occurs as a result of working with populations from different backgrounds. Students are out of their comfort zones and see injustice and inequity for the first time. As they interact with the people they are serving, they hear people telling their own stories. Putting a face on poverty breaks down stereotypes, and statistics become meaningful. Students become less judgmental and compassionate as they become more adept at perspective taking and considering chance's role in poverty situations.

Developing a greater awareness and broader perspective of social issues occurs through accurate information, constructive service experiences, and critical reflection. As students inform themselves on social, economic, and political issues, they question beliefs and assumptions that no longer provide adequate explanations for reality. Students develop a more critical, complex view of the world and begin to see how power relations limit options for oppressed groups. Students' increased understanding of social issues fosters an institutional, systemic view of the causes of injustice and inequity, where they may have only seen individual deficits.

Effective service-learning helps students see their potential to make change. Having many positive service experiences enhances their feelings of competency and *efficacy*. Doing important work that has real impact on people and the community develops a sense of *agency*—the belief that you can make a difference. Students develop an ethic of service and adopt it as part of their identity when they work with friends in a culture that values it. People who have a clear sense of their values are more likely to live in accordance with their beliefs, and individuals who regard service as a part of their identity are more likely to connect their personal commitment to service with a profession where they can make a social contribution.

Three Stages of White Critical-Consciousness Development
In addition to the set of essential elements of critical consciousness, another core component of the social-justice model of service-learning consists of the stages of White critical-consciousness development. Although those interviewed were committed to social justice, the survey responses represented a broad range of alumni experiences and attitudes. In reading the responses to the question "Why do you volunteer?" I had a nagging uneasiness with several answers and the terminology used. Responses like "It feels good to help the disadvantaged"; "I am so blessed, it's the least I can do"; or "All they really need is just a hand up"; led me to question the service providers' motivations and their views of the people they were serving. It seemed they were exploiting others for their own benefit and perpetuating an "us/them" mentality.

Yet having been a teacher at BSM for over thirty years, I knew many of the alumni to be generous, kind-hearted individuals who were just trying to help. After a dialogue with Dr. Eleni Roulis, my professor and critical friend, I began to view their responses as part of a journey traveled on the path to developing a critical consciousness.

While BSM has some socioeconomic diversity, the students are predominantly White and middle or upper-middle class. Therefore, my conclusions pertain particularly to the White experience of critical-consciousness development. Although students of color or those living in poverty would move through stages in a similar fashion, there would be different components due to their firsthand experiences with racism and classism.[19]

The initial stage of White critical-consciousness development through service-learning is *charity*. It is the natural point of departure for suburban students living in a segregated, racist society. Having minimal experience with diverse populations, racism, and discrimination, they uncritically internalize negative media messages about race and poverty. They want to help but have a limited view of the world. Being charitable is a good characteristic; but given the possibility that students might exploit mar-

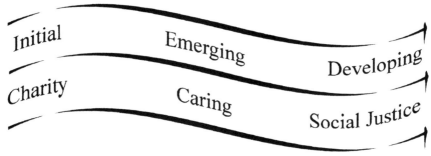

Figure 1.3.   Stages of White Critical Consciousness

ginalized populations for their own benefit, teachers should see this as only a first step and guide students into the next stage of critical-consciousness development: *caring*.

The emerging stage of White critical consciousness through service-learning is one of caring, and the catalyst to moving into this stage is relationship. As students interact with those they are serving, they develop *compassion*, see injustice, and question past beliefs. The dissonance between what they thought to be true and the reality they see makes them more aware of themselves, others, and social problems. If individuals are located in the caring stage for a period of time and care deeply about those they are serving, they become compelled to do something to change the system and move into the third stage of critical-consciousness development: *social justice*.

The developing stage of White critical consciousness is social justice. I have intentionally labeled this stage "developing" rather than "developed" because seeing others, the world, and ourselves clearly is a never-ending process. In the social-justice stage individuals make a lifelong commitment to work as *allies* with oppressed groups, to understand the root causes of injustice and take action to make the system more equitable.

Navigating the Stages of White Critical-Consciousness Development

The third component of the social-justice model for service-learning is a framework for teachers to help guide students on the path of becoming more critically aware. As they move through the stages of critical-consciousness development, students need stage-appropriate information, experience, and reflection for successful navigation. As educators, we create learning situations that initiate deeper self-exploration and critical analysis.

For students to navigate from the initial charity stage of critical consciousness to the caring stage, they need accurate information on those they

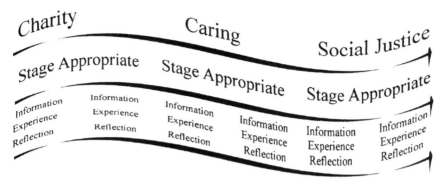

Figure 1.4. Navigating the Stages of White Critical Consciousness

serve and on social issues, such as homelessness, poverty, or the immigrant experience. Stage-appropriate service experiences include working in soup kitchens, homeless shelters, and food shelves. Student reflection should focus on clarifying their own values and obligation to others, as well as reflection on the current state of affairs and their vision for a better society.

In moving from a caring to a social-justice orientation to service, students need to investigate the social construction of race and the legacy of oppression in American institutions. This exploration also includes gaining a deeper awareness of White racial-identity development, White privilege, and the role of White antiracists. Service experiences should be in agencies that provide direct service as well as social-change advocacy. Students reflect on targets and agents of multiple systems of oppression (racism, sexism, classism, ageism, heterosexism, and others) and examine what they can do to combat oppression.

Once individuals develop a social-justice orientation to service, their task is to mature their critical consciousness. Information is needed to better understand the political and economic systems that perpetuate inequity and injustice. Service experiences are with advocacy, political, and/or grassroots agencies committed to transformative action. Reflection is centered on understanding how power and privilege operate to the advantage of the dominant class and to the exclusion of others.

It is important to acknowledge that critical-consciousness development progresses slowly over time and is not necessarily a linear process. Students often move between stages as they continue their service-learning journey, and individuals can be in more than one stage in different areas of their understanding. Realistically, given students' maturity levels and varied experiences, only some reach the developing stage by early adulthood. However, if students are equipped with critical-thinking skills, multiple service experiences, and a better understanding of themselves and the world, seeds are planted for continued growth toward critical consciousness.

Now it's time to find out more about how you can build a service-learning program robust enough to initiate and promote growth toward critical awareness and a commitment to social justice. Subsequent chapters offer a deeper understanding of the model and concrete strategies to use in the classroom. When teachers focus on social-justice education, they make a long-term commitment and accept an awesome responsibility to students and to society.

CHAPTER TWO

Becoming Committed to Service

This chapter describes the effects of early service experiences on adult attitudes and behaviors toward service and social justice. Using both quantitative and qualitative tools, I asked adults to reflect on their experiences and
capture in their own words the impact service work had on them. We will see
how these reflections not only highlight many positive outcomes of service-
learning experiences, but also lay a foundation for building service-learning
programs committed to social change.

By the Numbers: Effects of Early Service Experiences

High-School Service Experience

Regardless of the type of service program, individuals who participated in any
service during high school were more likely to volunteer extensively as adults
than those who did not. Likewise, they worked more often to promote social
justice and were more likely to volunteer for professional or work-related
organizations. Service participants reported that as a result of high-school
service activities, they developed a greater awareness of social problems, and
they clarified their values and identities as individuals.

Those who participated in an intense service experience, such as Peace
Corps, Americorps, residential missions, or service trips of a week or longer,
were more likely to promote and work for social justice as adults. As you
might expect, there is a growing trend of young people seeking out these
opportunities. Ten percent of the 1975–1994 alumni group volunteered in

an intense service program, compared to 25 percent of those graduating between 1995 and 1999.

Service-Learning Programs versus Community-Service Programs

Comparing the responses from students who participated in service-learning with those who participated in community service, we see differences
both in service experiences and in their understanding of social issues and
social justice. The experiences differed in the types of agencies where they
volunteered, the populations with whom they worked, and the frequency and
intensity of their work. When compared to community-service participants,
service-learning participants

- volunteered more at food shelves, soup kitchens, and homeless shelters;
- participated in more service projects initiated by themselves, family,
  or friends;
- participated in service more hours per month;
- participated more frequently in weeklong service experiences during
  high school.[1]

Participation in service-learning resulted in a more complex understanding of service, social issues, and poverty. These students had more direct
contact with people living in poverty and people from racial or ethnic groups
different from their own. They indicated that critical reflection and discussion on social justice was a component of their service experience, and they
developed a greater awareness of social problems; saw issues of discrimination and poverty as a societal problem rather than as individual deficits; and
worked with adults committed to promoting social justice for all citizens.

By the People: Effects of Early Service Experiences

In the survey I asked alumni for reflections: "What did you learn from your
service experience, which you would like to pass on to a young person
just starting out?" and "What impact has your early service experience
had on your behavior and attitude toward service and social justice?" In
their responses, alumni spoke about how the experiences impacted their
personal growth, values, and identity. They also reflected on the role service played in developing their worldviews and awareness of people with
diverse backgrounds.

Table 2.1 is a summary of themes drawn from their collective memories, providing evidence of service's positive outcomes. As we walk through their reflections, I include individual quotations demonstrating how they internalized the experiences. You will notice that their responses reflect different orientations to service. Some descriptions clearly denote a charity outlook, others demonstrate a caring attitude, and several reveal a commitment to social justice.

Table 2.1. Outcomes of Early Service Experiences

INCREASED SELF-AWARENESS AND THE ABILITY TO MAKE A DIFFERENCE

Students
- learn more about themselves and develop confidence;
- gain a sense of empowerment and realize their potential to make a difference;
- clarify their values;
- realize their capacity to give and develop patience and compassion;
- become less materialistic and more appreciative of what they have;
- gain a better perspective of their lives;
- come to recognize their own privilege;
- develop skills and interests that lead to career paths;
- develop an ethic of service which continues through adulthood;
- develop a commitment to the larger community;
- become more politically aware and develop a commitment to act.

INCREASED AWARENESS OF OTHERS

Students
- learn about people whose experiences and backgrounds are different from theirs;
- gain a better understanding of perspectives and diversity;
- become more open-minded and less judgmental;
- develop an understanding of themselves in relation to others.

INCREASED AWARENESS OF SOCIAL ISSUES

Students
- become more aware of social issues;
- can identify different perspectives on reality;
- develop a deeper understanding of social justice;
- have a more complex understanding of the current situations and the need to look for political solutions;
- may participate in service abroad and thereby develop a global awareness of poverty, and see themselves connected to others worldwide.

Increased Self-Awareness and the Ability to Make a Difference

Alumni overwhelmingly saw their service experiences as positive and enjoyable, noting that volunteering made them feel good about themselves. They also recognized the reciprocal nature of service and how they often received more than they gave, learning more about themselves and developing confidence. They gained a sense of empowerment and realized their potential to make a difference in the world. Not only did society benefit from their service, but being role models often led others into service.

- "The personal satisfaction and the rewards are priceless. I volunteer more now than ever because I enjoy it so much."
- "[Volunteering] may be uncomfortable at first, but the rewards are worth the effort. Volunteerism makes you feel good about yourself at the time and helps to build good character. It helped me break out of my shyness."
- "Serving is an opportunity, so it is imperative for volunteers to realize that while they are giving their time and expertise, they are also taking from the people and the situation in so many different ways."
- "It can contribute to developing yourself, your confidence, and how it can impact your interests and career path."
- "One person, one deed, one interaction can make a difference."
- "I've learned that even one person can make a difference. Volunteering has a snowball effect—you can influence others to become involved and have a cause. No matter how small a contribution of time you make, it can significantly impact others."

Service involvement changes students and helps clarify their values. They realize their capacity to give, and they learn patience and compassion. Many responses include phrases such as "more compassionate," "*empathy* to others," and "consideration or concern for others." For example, one woman noted, "In a way it has influenced me in the way I deal with people. I work in criminal justice and it has made me more compassionate." Another described how service activities "increased my patience and understanding of people different than myself."

- "Volunteering aided in my growth and development as a young adult. Also I feel my values and morals were highly influenced by this experience."
- "One week as a counselor at a camp for the mentally handicapped made me realize how much I could give and how easy life for me is."

As a result of their service, students became less materialistic and more appreciative of what they had, often gaining a new perspective on their own lives: "My service made me appreciate the life that I had, even though I knew some of my friends had a lot more than I did. It put things in perspective." Alumni saw service for young people as particularly important, noting that "high school and adolescence in general can cause people to fixate on their own tiny world." Service "puts you in the habit of looking past only yourself," making you "think with a wider view; not everyone has the same privilege."

Students' personal values change through mission trip experiences, as they come to realize their own privilege and become more open-minded and nonjudgmental:

- "Before traveling to Mexico for my first time with the school mission trip, I was very attached to physical things and 'security.' When I saw the joy and freedom from stuff and the ability to share (even when it hurt) that those very poor people had, I lost my love for 'things.' I wanted what they had."

Through service, students often develop skills and interests leading to different career paths. The "positive experiences and a sense of confidence" led one graduate to change his path to human services and to volunteer for the Peace Corps. Similarly, many are drawn to helping fields as a result of their early experiences in service. Nurses, teachers, and individuals working in the justice system described how volunteering influenced them in their work, making them more compassionate and understanding of diversity, and giving them the ability to see issues in more complex ways.

- "The majority of my volunteer work was hospital-related. It brought out something I didn't know I had—the want to help. I became a nurse."
- "I think my volunteering/service greatly affected my career path and decision to be a pediatrician. In medicine, you serve people every day as your profession and often see injustices and can try to change them. You are an advocate for your patients—in my case children. I'm fortunate that I found a profession that melds my love of science and learning with my love of service."

Service becomes a part of students' identity; they come to see volunteering as part of who they are and what they do. Phrases such as "a pattern for life," "part of my way of life," or the double negative "I can't imagine not volunteering," illustrate the profound influence that service has on identity formation, connecting early service experience and life choices.

- "At the very least, it instilled in me a commitment to the larger community that should be reflected in the way I live my life with or without volunteer work."
- "In high school, being involved in service activities was the norm. Now it feels unnatural not to be volunteering in some fashion."

Service also impacts students' political formation. Many alumni described themselves as having become more liberal, wanting to influence social issues, and believing in the "power and importance of people organizing, lobbying, and working for social justice." Service has the potential to broaden political awareness and the commitment to act.

- "Service experiences have instilled a strong desire . . . to do whatever I can to help those without a voice be heard."
- "I have a greater awareness of the world we live in. It shaped my political beliefs and fosters a commitment to justice and equality for all persons regardless of race, religion, sexual orientation."

Early service experiences greatly influence adult service because they create openness and a willingness to continue service, as seen in comments such as "opened the door to something that I eagerly continue," "laid the groundwork for future involvement," and "planted a seed." For others these experiences "took the mystery of community service away," and were instrumental in "breaking the ice and opening my willingness to 'get out there.'" A final comment is representative of the message conveyed by many: "Early service shaped my attitude and provided the foundation that I have continued into adulthood."

Increased Awareness of Others

Early service experiences help students learn about different people, "opening their eyes," and making them more open-minded, and this wider view results in a better understanding and less judgment.

- "It has helped me understand different backgrounds that my students come from and allows me to reach them more effectively."
- "My service taught me about other identities and ideas. It taught me to be open-minded."

- "When you attend BSM or just live in the suburbs, it becomes easy to believe that everyone drives an SUV, that you are poor if you make $75,000. Service takes you out of the bubble. It gives you perspective."
- "It opened my eyes to the world outside of my protected suburban life. People struggle daily and are in situations which are outside of their control. Volunteering can educate someone about the poor or disabled or addicted in ways that the media cannot."

This increased awareness of perspectives and diversity and the deeper understanding of others is a result of "getting out of their comfort zone." While there may be some initial fear, it gets easier over time.

- "Getting out of your comfort zone is a great experience. Interacting with people, places and events that you normally don't come across is an excellent way to determine what is actually important to you and is a big wake-up call in regards to what is and is not working correctly in this country."

This teaches students about themselves in relation to others and opens them up to different situations. As one person counseled, it is all right to feel uncomfortable and "find you have some 'unspeakable' prejudice against people who are drunks, or poor, or minority . . . it happens to everyone," and young people should continue volunteering and work through it.

While many alumni felt they were more open-minded and had a greater understanding of diverse populations, they often had differing views of those served. Those with a charity orientation to service used words such as "disadvantaged" and "needy," illustrating a deficit view of those they helped. Others revealed a more caring attitude, noting that they could see themselves in the same situation. Expressions like "stepping into someone else's shoes" and "there but for the grace of God, go I" indicate an ability to imagine life from other perspectives.

- "When working with people society considers 'less fortunate' or 'disadvantaged,' remember we are all two steps away from being in their place—it can happen to anyone."

The third group of responses reflects a social-justice orientation. They show "an awareness of human worth and dignity of others regardless of their lot in life" and express understanding of the equality of all, despite different life circumstances.

- "It took me awhile to realize that there is a difference in attitude in volunteering as an 'advantaged' person to 'disadvantaged' people and being a person simply who is in a current place to help another person who needs it at the time."
- "More than anything I came to learn enough to understand Ani DiFranco's song lyrics. 'If I were you, you are just who I'd be.' Life's circumstances are not character flaws. You can't judge people who have faced challenges you have not."

Increased Awareness of Social Issues

Early service experiences give students an increased awareness of social issues and a new perspective on reality. One individual explained that she "was raised thinking everybody had the same amount as myself and those in my neighborhood" and through volunteering saw that was not the case. Volunteering gives "a better perspective on some of the challenges that exist in a community—poverty, broken homes, low literacy rates." Many expressed new understandings with comments such as "Life isn't fair, and people don't always get what they deserve," and "It made me see or seek out the other side of societal ills. I realize that things aren't always what they seem, that there are gray areas."

Early service experiences also lead to a deeper understanding of social justice and the understanding of the potential for change given supportive measures.

- "My experiences helped me see more societal problems and helped me to realize the importance of social justice."
- "It embedded the importance of serving others into my value system and increased my awareness of social issues. It has taught me that all people can lead productive lives if we are accepting and supportive in our attitudes and actions with others."

One alumna noted that she applied her early service experiences to college classes on social justice: "I feel that because of my experiences, I have a greater capacity to critically think about social justices and injustices."

The awareness of social justice is reflected in a more complex understanding of the situation and the need to look for political solutions. Many alumni offered opinions on "how our country should be run" and the role of government.

- "My experiences helped me realize that there are so many disenfranchised people in this country for whatever reasons. You learn that it is not fair or appropriate to blame individuals for their poverty or other problems. Somewhere along the line the community or the government has failed them. Our task is to rebuild social safety nets for these people while also helping them to be more accountable for their decisions and actions."

- "I realized that there are more people than ever who needed aid . . . I think it shows me that government programs, not only volunteer groups or non-profits, need to be put in place because then every socio-economic group would be given basic needs such as health care."

Service experiences abroad provide a global view of poverty and have a powerful impact on students. They contribute to seeing themselves, "not only as an individual, but as a part of the world and thus a responsible contributor to it."

- "Social justice is a world-wide and complex issue that will need to be addressed indefinitely."
- "It would be difficult to measure the impact on my life. All my experiences were incredible. I think because my service was mainly focused outside of the U.S., it has given me a wide understanding of our country and the impact we have to other countries and people with regard to social justice."

In summary, adults reflecting on their early service experiences frequently described the impact on their behavior and attitude toward service and social justice as increasing their awareness and understanding of themselves and their potential to make change, as well as building a broader perspective of other people and the world. These quotes illustrate that service-learning programs, when designed and delivered effectively with an emphasis on critical pedagogy, play a crucial role in developing citizens engaged for the common good. Chapter 3 delves into how social-justice service-learning affects individuals, providing a foundation on which to build better programs.

CHAPTER THREE

Becoming Committed
to Social Justice

The challenge for teachers who are building a social-justice service-learning program is to understand how individuals become committed to social change. Through my research, I have identified common experiences, attitudes, and behaviors of people working for social justice, providing a framework for service-learning programs that foster long-term civic engagement for equity and justice. By examining this set of characteristics, we are one step further on our journey.

This chapter is based on the reflections of eleven alumni from Benilde-St. Margaret's School (BSM) gathered during individual interviews about their experiences with service and social justice. Their profiles provide living evidence of what we hope to achieve through social-justice service-learning programs.

In their current jobs or professions, these individuals indicate a connection between their careers and their commitment to social justice. Some of them work with social-service agencies where personal and professional services are intertwined with social justice. Others use their professional advocacy careers to advance social causes and youth development, and still others create social-justice opportunities by using business skills to effect social change. More than half are politically engaged or have advocacy roles in their service activities.

In addition to the service/social-justice component of their jobs, many individuals continue to devote time to regular service activities, and all continue to work in varying degrees with agencies serving populations living in

Table 3.1. Common Experiences of Adults Committed to Social Justice

Family
- Their families instilled values and modeled service.
- They had a family situation that made them feel different from their peers.
- They had a broader, more inclusive definition of *family*.

Educational Environment
- Values were both taught and modeled in their schools.
- Their classes provided opportunities to explore and discuss their beliefs and obligations to others.
- Their schools' missions included a commitment to service and social justice.
- Their schools provided a mentoring environment.

Common Service Experiences
- They had extensive service experiences in multiple sites.
- They had leadership roles in designing and implementing service projects.
- They worked directly with people from different backgrounds.
- They enjoyed service and participated in service with their friends.
- They worked alongside adults committed to social justice.
- They had service experiences abroad.

poverty. Additionally, they volunteer in the community with youth groups and in educational institutions, as well as through their professions in work-related organizations.

The commonalities from their personal stories give us insight into key ingredients that contribute to forming an action identity committed to justice. After exploring their experiences growing up, we see how their background contributed to their identity formation and their commitment to social justice. In the final section of this chapter, we broaden our understanding by connecting these findings to other research on the characteristics of social-justice activists, identity formation, and the role of mentoring institutions.

Common Characteristics of Individuals Committed to Social Justice

Family
It's no surprise that the family functions as the first teacher for most children, communicating on a daily basis what is valued and expected both through words and actions.[1] When parents are committed to service in the community, children receive the message that helping others is important.

In describing their families, all my interviewees discussed influences that instilled values and modeled service. Many had their first service experiences with their mothers or other family members, volunteering at church, in nursing homes, and in the community. This laid the foundation for service to become part of their identities.

As they gave details about their childhoods, I noted that each person mentioned a family situation or trait that made him or her feel different from peers. Many had family structures that represented a broader, more inclusive definition of *family*. Several families had adopted children, some from other racial and ethnic groups, and two had multigenerational or extended-family living situations. Some people mentioned divorces, remarriages, and step-families. Other situations included parents with issues of mental illness and chemical-abuse treatment. While these circumstances are more common today, it was not the case growing up during the 1960s, 1970s, and 1980s.

Having a family structure or circumstance that varies from their peers' gives children an experience with difference, as they learn the meanings of *in-group* and *out-group*. This early personal relationship with "otherness" builds their capacity for empathy and compassion and results in a more inclusive view of others. The broader view of what constitutes "family" allows children to see that their caring circle can be expanded to include new people to whom they have become connected.

Teachers know that families are important, but they often have very little control over what is happening at home, and they may have limited knowledge about individual students' family lives. While a family background that instills service as a core value is important for creating an orientation to social justice, many students will develop a thirst for social justice regardless of their early family experiences.

Educational Experience

In addition to families, schools and religious organizations send messages to young people about norms, values, and expected behavior,[2] and they play a critical role in developing students' moral and civic identities. Many interviewees said the values that were both taught and modeled in their schools were important factors in their formation. Seven attended Catholic elementary schools, all attended BSM Catholic high school, and nine attended a Catholic postbaccalaureate institution. They recalled teachers who spoke about their community involvement and service activities, such as Peace Corps and mission work. In public institutions, teachers participating in service activities are also in a position to incorporate their stories and experiences into the curriculum, as long as they avoid including religious missions.

A school's mission is a major factor in the development of students' social justice orientation during their formative years. The interviewees' high school is committed to educate within a framework of Christian values and to develop students in mind, body, and spirit. Students are challenged to choose ethical and moral courses of action and to act in accordance with their beliefs through charity, works for justice, and service to others.

Looking back, interviewees described their religion classes as opportunities to explore their faith and their obligation to others. Theology classes provide students opportunities to take time for reflection about values and beliefs and to have conversations on important issues, such as the meaning of living a moral, ethical life. Teachers and coaches are encouraged to talk about values and describe their own service experiences here and abroad. These interactions can be catalysts for students to expand their view of possibilities and obligations and to think about how they can make a difference. In secular institutions, the basic tenets of humanism can be incorporated into social studies, history, civics, and government classes. Discussions of ethics and morality are vital to schools' democratic mission.

Through high school and college, young people's developmental task is to define their identities.[3] They are at a point in their lives when they have to make conscious choices and decisions about beliefs, abilities, and their philosophy of life. During this developmental phase, students need a supportive community where they can grapple with important life questions such as who am I? where do I belong? who do I want to become? and what is life all about? Encouraging students to ask big questions and think critically creates an environment that is supportive of their search for meaning and purpose.[4]

Teachers can encourage students to think about their place in the world by using the Socratic method of questioning. Simply asking why, how, or what in relation to the subject matter can create interesting and revealing discussions that delve deeper into the topic at hand and connect it to the students' lives and the world outside the classroom.

Common Service Experiences

A significant ingredient of these alumni's service experiences is that they had multiple experiences at many sites. They worked directly with people from different backgrounds, participated in service with their friends, and worked alongside adults committed to social justice.

High School

Nearly all interviewees participated in service during high school. They provided service to the school and wider community through classes, churches, civic groups, and school clubs. Many assumed leadership roles in initiating service projects. Tutoring at school or at other institutions was a common activity, and food shelves, homeless centers, nursing homes, and hospitals were other volunteer sites. The majority of these students worked directly with diverse populations in their service activities. Several named teachers who were instrumental in getting them involved in service.

Reflecting on the high-school service experience, they realized that it helped them overcome their fear of people with different backgrounds and circumstances and laid the groundwork for future service. Venturing into new territories with new people and performing meaningful work developed their feelings of being capable and making a difference.

Participating in service with their peers was also a common thread contributing to becoming more comfortable in diverse settings. They commented that working with their friends made service activities an enjoyable, natural activity, stating, "It's just what we did."

College

All eleven participated in service during their college years, although their service experiences varied a great deal in frequency and intensity. Many individuals mentioned a service center on campus that helped facilitate service experiences, and two continued to engage in service activities organized by their college alumni groups. The three alumni who were most involved in service and social justice attended Jesuit universities. They clearly stated that service was part of the mission, integrated into the school's cultures and course work, and an expectation of all students.

Service Experiences Abroad

Nine of the interviewees lived, studied, or volunteered overseas for varying lengths of time and with varying frequency, ranging from one week to two years and from one to seven times throughout their youth and postcollege years. These experiences impacted their understanding of themselves and the world. In addition to overseas experiences, two had full-time yearlong commitments to service programs in the United States.

Organizations

In describing their service history and their current service activities, all interviewees indicated that they worked directly with people living in poverty. In addition, they volunteered at similar types of organizations, in three general areas: those serving marginalized persons living in poverty or crisis, such as food shelves, shelters, and housing programs; youth-development programs, youth-in-crisis programs, and tutoring programs serving urban poor or students who had recently immigrated; and overseas service programs. Several also provided services to individuals with physical or mental challenges. Many were involved in civic committees or participated in political or social-advocacy work. Other sites of volunteer work mentioned were hospitals and nursing homes, places of worship, and their high school and colleges.

Transforming Experiences into Identity

In synthesizing the common experiences of these individuals, several components emerge as important factors in forming their identities and their social-justice orientation to service: multiple, enjoyable service opportunities with family and friends; the design of school-based service experiences; and working with diverse populations. How do these early experiences impact who they become as adults?

Multiple opportunities for service work in high school and young adult-hood, along with parental and school role models, instill the value of service to others and create an ethic of service. The fact that students enjoy service work and participate in activities with friends reinforces the positive nature of service, and it becomes a part of who they are, as illustrated by the double negative stated by more than one person, "I couldn't not do it."

The design and implementation of school-based experiences are important factors in developing a social-justice orientation to service. Students at BSM are required to take one of the religion classes that incorporate Catholic social teachings; choices include two service-learning classes and an advocacy-based class. The students volunteer with agencies serving marginalized populations, most frequently with people living in poverty or people living with mental or physical challenges. Having service experiences embedded in courses provides a structure for students to better prepare for the experience with accurate information and ample time for critical reflection before, during, and after the service activity.

Researching social problems and discussing moral issues—such as humanity's obligation to the common good, care for the poor, and the dignity and rights of all people—help students develop a clearer view of the underlying causes of poverty and a stronger sense of their responsibility to others. With time devoted to both inward reflection, asking, "What effect did this experience have on me?" and outward reflection, asking, "Why does this situation exist?" and "How do my actions work for or against change?" students begin to see their potential to make change.

In students' quest for identity, they look for others who are like them and have the same values. When service programs are designed to encourage peers to work alongside each other on projects that they have developed, they see it as both a fun and a meaningful activity. The collegiality surrounding the service experience is continued after high school and college into adulthood. Service programs that create leadership opportunities reinforce students in conceiving of themselves as capable and effective and increase their independence and self-directedness.

Working with diverse populations impacts students' orientation to service. While diversity exists at BSM, the majority of the students are of similar socioeconomic and racial backgrounds. In order for these students to develop a commitment to social justice, they need to experience diversity and be in relationships with individuals from different backgrounds and circumstances. Not only does this, along with accurate information and reflection, break down stereotypes, it puts a human face on suffering and fosters care and compassion. These encounters dismantle the wall between "us" and "them."

Travel, studying, and/or serving in other cultures provide additional opportunities for students to learn about themselves, others, and sociopolitical issues. Seeing other ways of being, knowing, and living spurs individuals to reassess their own values, beliefs, and knowledge. Positive interactions develop a sense of connectedness and increase their ability to see the complexity and interrelatedness of economic, social, and political situations. With opportunities for reflection and social analysis, students begin to see how those with power organize information and direct events to maintain the status quo.

Deepening Our Understanding of Identity Formation

We have seen how individuals' backgrounds and experiences contribute to their adult orientation to social justice. Not only do these findings hold true for this particular group of adults, but other authors have found similar results with different populations. Additionally, by connecting what we have learned in this chapter to other research on socialization, identity formation, and the impact of educational institutions, we deepen our understanding of how individuals become committed to social justice.

Commonalities of People Committed to Social Justice
In *Common Fire*, Laurent A. Daloz and others conducted a study in which they interviewed more than one hundred adults who had made long-term commitments to work for the common good. They found these individuals

- had parents who were active in the public sphere;
- had a strong sense of self-esteem and a feeling they could make a difference;

- recognized justice and injustice and saw the contradictions between espoused values and reality;
- had traveled significantly in young adulthood.

Their commitment to the common good was strengthened through their communities, peer groups, and mentors. They also had opportunities to increase their leadership skills during their teen years. They developed compassion and changed their opinion of who is "one of us" through constructive engagement with otherness. The interviewees maintained the conviction that everyone counts and recognized resemblance in difference as a fact.[5]

Likewise, Stanton, Giles, and Cruz, in *Service-Learning: A Movement's Pioneers Reflect on its Origins, Practice, and Future*, examined the characteristics of early service-learning teachers and found commonalities that planted seeds of commitment for moral and civic engagement. Parental role models as volunteers and activists, connection to school life, a family-centered community, and a coming of age during the turbulent times of the 1950s, 1960s, or 1970s were common elements in their development. In addition, they had inquiring minds and questioned the meaning of family, society, and education.

Service-learning pioneers were committed to service both on the individual level of helping people in need and on the societal level, which was nurtured by role models, challenging friends, and critical events. They had a strong sense of themselves and their ability to have an impact; strong religious, ethical, or spiritual motivations; and well-developed political convictions. Findings also showed visionary passion and commitment, compassion, and self-directed independence as common characteristics.[6]

Identity Formation
Students learn about themselves through introspection, reflection on how others see them, comparison of themselves to others, and memories of past experiences. Family, individuals, groups, and society influence their identity development. The social context is important as young people's worlds expand beyond their immediate families to the broader culture, and they come to see themselves in a larger context.[7] How individuals view themselves includes past experiences, what they currently think about themselves, and what they see as possibilities. They construct their images of their future selves from models of what they hope to become and those they want to avoid.[8]

Miranda Yates and James Youniss present an updated theory on socialization in *Roots of Civic Identity: International Perspectives on Community Service and Activism in Youth.* They explain that in the past we thought socialization was simply the internalizing of societies' norms and values, a conception that depicted youth as passive receptacles, receiving culture from adults. Now we recognize youth as active participants in organizing and making sense of messages sent by adults and institutions. Socialization involves a cognitive process and the acquisition of practices that become "habitual ways of acting that are part of a person's self-concept or, more accurately, essential components of a person's identity."[9]

The authors determined that active experiences lead to habitual practices, which become part of one's identity.[10] For example, they found that the strongest predictor of adult involvement in democratic practices is participation in student government. Similarly, they report that students and adults who are active in service see their actions as a part of who they are and not as something unusual or meriting recognition. Their results also state that community service-learning instills habits of political participation in students.[11]

Individuals' sense of identity determines their course of action and motivates them to behave in accordance with their values. Young people's identities develop over time as they reflect on and question their beliefs and assumptions. Identity formation also occurs as a result of identification with role models. Service-learning encourages youth to investigate and discuss social, moral, and political issues and reflect on their responsibilities and obligations.[12]

Moral and Political Development

In *Educating Citizens: Preparing America's Undergraduates for Lives of Moral and Civic Responsibility*, Anne Colby and others investigate the process of identity formation, including the connection between self-knowledge and one's moral and political development. They describe the interconnectedness between moral development (judgments about how to treat others) and civic principles of democracy, such as respect, tolerance, and the rights of both individuals and groups. Likewise, engaging in civic activities, like promoting access to housing or health care, or drawing attention to environmental concerns, always includes moral considerations.[13]

These researchers conclude that developing engaged moral and civic individuals requires a moral and civic understanding that includes a knowledge of complex issues and institutions, as well as ethical and democratic principles; the motivation, conviction, and perseverance to act morally and ethically; and the necessary skills in communication and political participation, and the ability to work with people and organize them for action.

The motivation to act requires a strong sense of self and efficacy. Colby and colleagues also note that in addition to caring about the issues and being involved, civically active individuals need to feel it is possible for them to make a difference. That is to say, they need to have both personal and political efficacy in order to effectively engage in the political process.[14]

Service-learning is one of the strategies used by institutions committed to developing students with moral and civic responsibility. Yates and Youniss found strong evidence that youths' civic engagement can result in the formation of political habits that are integrated into their identity, continue into adulthood, and shape how they see their role in society. The long-term impact of early service experience results from students seeing themselves as "politically engaged and socially concerned person[s], . . . [with a] sense of social agency and responsibility for society and political-moral awareness."[15]

Mentoring Institutions

Sharon Daloz Parks, in *Big Questions, Worthy Dreams: Mentoring Young Adults in their Search for Meaning, Purpose, and Faith*, describes the characteristics of mentoring institutions that assist students in identity formation. Noting that the overused term *mentor* can have many meanings, she restricts its meaning to "those who are appropriately depended upon for authoritative guidance at the time of the development of critical thought and the formation of an informed, adult, and committed faith."[16] She describes a mentor as the person who recognizes you and your potential, supports you in your journey, challenges you to be critical, and inspires you to meaningful commitment.

Educational institutions can provide mentors and a mentoring environment that encourages students to ask big questions and think critically. Parks identifies seven characteristics of a mentoring institution:

- being a network of belonging where young adults feel at home physically, emotionally, intellectually, and spiritually;
- asking the big questions, which stretch students in their thinking about themselves and social arrangements;
- providing opportunities for constructive encounters with otherness, which create bonds transcending "us and them" to a new "we" and a commitment to common good;
- promoting habits of mind that encompass dialogue, critical thought, connected-holistic thought, and contemplation;
- fostering worthy dreams in which students imagine possibilities and find a vocation which adds meaning and purpose to their lives;

- providing access to images including the truth of a world of suffering and wonder, positive self-images, images of others both as similar and unique, and images of interconnectedness;
- creating communities of humanizing practices where the hearth gives students balance and invites dialogue and reflection, where the table always has a place for all to share, accommodate, and be grateful, and where the commons provides a space for the community to stand up, and to stand with others over time.[17]

Colby and others also conducted research on the ability of educational institutions to impact student moral and civic identity. They studied twelve institutions of higher education, including public and private, that are intentional in providing moral and civic education to students, defined as

> imparting the understanding that it is important to be generous and responsible to our family, friends, and neighbors . . . [and] responsible, responsive, patriotic, and loyal to our nation and society . . . [and to acknowledge that] educated citizens must understand and accept their obligations to all humanity, to making this a nation worth defending in a world safe and promising for all its inhabitants.[18]

Common features among these universities include integrating moral and civic education into the curriculum, often tying it to critical thinking, and teaching effective communication for civil discourse. They design activities that move students beyond the classroom and help them to see themselves as citizens, which raises their sense of efficacy and incorporates moral and civic action into their identity. These institutions also link moral and civic education with issues of diversity and multiculturalism, to foster respect for difference and develop a global perspective. Three themes that emerge are connections with communities, moral and civic virtue, and concerns for social justice.[19]

In identifying common themes from the stories and experiences of eleven individuals committed to social justice and linking them to findings from other research, we begin to understand how well-designed programs can help individuals develop a social-justice orientation to service. Important elements include understanding the characteristics of people committed to social justice, understanding the process of identity formation, and understanding the potential of mentoring institutions. Service experiences embedded in educational settings can foster an ethic of service and increased awareness of self, others, and social issues, resulting in individuals developing a more critical consciousness, a motivation to create change, and a lifelong commitment to social justice.

CHAPTER FOUR

Developing a Critical Consciousness

Four Elements of Critical-Consciousness Development

How can service-learning become transformative in nature and develop engaged citizens working for social change? The short answer is: *through developing a more critical consciousness.* There are four essential elements that contribute to critical-consciousness development: developing a deeper awareness of self, developing a deeper awareness and broader perspective of others, developing a deeper awareness and broader perspective of social issues, and seeing one's potential to make change. However, service experiences alone will not generate a commitment to social justice. We need to be intentional in the mission and design of the service program and create opportunities for students to grow in each of these four areas. Teachers must also work to become critically aware so that we can better guide our students in developing a critical consciousness.

Developing a Greater Awareness of Self

Effective service-learning opportunities help students develop a strong sense of self, giving them a sense that what they are doing is important. The ethic of service becomes a component of how they see themselves. Service experiences that are designed to give students opportunities to set goals, implement plans, and persist in their efforts increase their feelings of competency and efficacy. Doing work that has real impact on people and the community fosters a sense of agency and the belief that they can affect change. Additionally,

Figure 4.1.   Four Elements of Critical Consciousness Development

when students take on leadership roles in service activities, it reinforces their self-image as capable and effective and increases their creativity, independence, and self-directedness.

Well-designed service programs encourage peers to collaborate on projects so they can realize helping others is both an enjoyable and a meaningful activity. Working with their friends is key for students because in searching for their own identity, they frequently look to others who are like them and have the similar values. High school and college peers who participate together in service activities often continue their commitment of service into adulthood.

Students become more aware of themselves as they clarify their values through reflection, discussion, and actions. Skillfully designed assignments and discussion provoke students to think about who they are now, who they want to become, how they will act, and what will be important to them. These discussions also contribute to their understanding of civic responsibility and a moral obligation to work for social justice.

Another element that helps students clarify their values is working with adults who are committed to social justice. Their parents, teachers, friends, and other adults who are working in service agencies addressing social issues are sources of inspiration, challenging them in their thinking and actions. Mentors and adults outside family relationships provide an objective affirmation of the value of service and the confirmation that everyone is responsible for the common good. Students learn from these role models and come to identify with their values.

Students are increasingly seeking service opportunities away from their familiar surroundings. Often organized by schools, colleges, or religious organizations, these experiences include international travel or travel to impoverished communities within the United States. These experiences not only increase students' understanding about themselves, but also expand their awareness of others and knowledge of social issues.

Developing a Greater Awareness of Others

Often students' experience with otherness begins in their early years as a personal encounter with being different from their peers. Having a family situation or personal characteristic that sets them apart results in learning the meaning of *in-group* and *out-group*. This experience lays the groundwork for seeing diversity and developing compassion for others.

Most middle- and upper-class White students spend the majority of their time with people of similar socioeconomic and racial backgrounds. In order for these students to develop a commitment to social justice, they need to experience diversity and be in relationships with people who have different life experiences. Not only does this break down stereotypes but, along with accurate information and reflection, it puts a human face on suffering, fostering care and compassion. These encounters dismantle the wall between "us" and "them."

Students' self-awareness and awareness of others increase as they work with agencies serving diverse populations. Working with people from different ethnic or racial backgrounds, people living in poverty, or individuals with physical or mental challenges initiates a student's exploration of difference, similarity, and diversity within inclusiveness. Students come to see people as individuals with their own stories, rather than as statistics and stereotypes. Through these experiences, students recognize other ways of living and thinking, which encourages them to be more open-minded and to see the world from other perspectives.

Encounters with otherness help students overcome their fear of the unknown and lay the foundation for future social-justice work. Understanding the significant role that circumstances, which are often beyond one's control, play in people's lives allows students to see how misfortunes could befall anyone. As students create relationships with diverse people, it opens avenues of caring, *empathy* (the ability to understand and share another's feelings), and *compassion* (a general sense of responsibility and tendency to make commitments).[1] Reflection promotes a sense of interconnectedness between people and a will to act to relieve suffering.

Developing a Greater Awareness of Social Issues

Accurate information, constructive service experiences, and critical reflection develop students' critical consciousness of the world. When students become more aware and informed about sociopolitical issues, they realize that what they had previously believed is often inaccurate. Those beliefs no longer adequately explain the reality they see through their service work with diverse populations and communities.

Students see the contradictions between what they (and society) say they value and believe in and the injustices they see others experiencing. This creates a dissonance that destabilizes their worldview and leads to self-examination and questioning. Given new information and opportunities for reflection and analysis, students accommodate new knowledge and develop a critical, complex view of the world. As students build relationships and gain perspective, they see how power affects political decisions and limits options for oppressed groups, which contributes to their understanding of institutional, rather than individual, causes of injustice.

While students need only travel fifteen minutes to see examples of injustice and people living in poverty in their own communities, having a study or service experience abroad can have a powerful impact on how students think about themselves, others, and sociopolitical issues. Seeing the reality of economically disadvantaged people overseas sparks students' reappraisal of their values, beliefs, and knowledge. Positive encounters continue to develop their sense of connectedness with others and increase students' ability to see the complexity and interrelatedness of economic, social, and political situations. With opportunities for reflection and social analysis, they begin to see how government and policy decisions in the United States affect other countries and peoples.

Seeing One's Potential to Make Change

Once students understand that the world is more complex and social problems are more widespread than they thought, service-learning becomes a vehicle for acting on their beliefs and making a difference. Witnessing poverty, discrimination, and injustice presents an opportunity for students to step back and compare their privileged world with that of others and question, Why? This often leads to more research and analysis and contributes to students' political formation and commitment to civic engagement.

The double negative used by several alumni in talking about service: "I couldn't not do it" illustrates the long-term impact on students who value the camaraderie of service when participating with friends. This is one strong reason why providing multiple service opportunities in their high school and college years helps to instill the value of service to others. These early peer service opportunities coupled with parental and school role models create an ethic of service that continues throughout their adult years.

As a result of discussion and reflection around the questions, "Who am I?" and "Why am I here?" in conjunction with "Why are there social problems and injustices?" students develop a commitment to the common good and praxis for social justice. People who have a clear sense of their values and who see service as a part of their identity are more likely to live in accordance with their beliefs. They also tend to connect their personal commitments to service with jobs or professions where they can make a social contribution.

Three Stages of White Critical-Consciousness Development

As students grow in their ability to see themselves and the world more clearly, their views and orientation to service change as reflected in a three-stage model of White critical-consciousness development. The initial stage of consciousness—charity—is a natural point of departure for many White, middle- and upper-class students who have little experience with discrimination, poverty, or diverse racial and ethnic groups. In the second stage, students' worldviews are emerging, and their service orientation evolves into caring about those they are helping. The final stage of White critical consciousness incorporates an understanding of the underlying causes of injustice and a commitment to work for social change. To understand these stages and the importance of helping students foster a critical stance to their

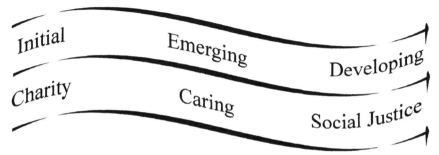

Figure 4.2. Stages of White Critical Consciousness Development

service experiences, we need to address some fundamental issues regarding charity, caring, and social justice.

Is Charity Bad?

Is charity bad? Of course not. Charity, as described by Merriam-Webster, is commonly understood as "generosity and helpfulness, especially toward the needy or suffering," is a necessary component of our society and the human experience, and there are many schools and organizations that contribute to their communities through charitable projects such as food drives, fundraising, raking yards for the elderly, tutoring, helping with youth clubs, and environmental work.

Research indicates that altruism—helping others without any expectation of personal benefit—is an innate part of human nature. Felix Warneken and Michael Tomasello report altruism in infants as young as eighteen months. Twenty-four toddlers were presented with an adult male experimenter who encountered a problem, such as dropping an object he could not reach or knocking over books. Without the adult looking at or speaking to the child, the infant got up and helped the adult. Of note was that the child only helped complete the task if the experimenter seemed upset at not being able to reach his goal.[2] Indeed, if the desire to help others is imprinted on our human nature, what is problematic about charitable service-learning programs?

The charity-or-justice debate is a major tension among service-learning advocates. Teachers and administrators question whether service-learning programs should be apolitical or a vehicle to engage students in political, economic, and social issues. Questions raised over a decade ago, such as what are the goals of the program? whose values are being promoted? whose needs are being met? and who is doing what to whom and for what reason?[3] are still relevant today. The answers to these questions guide the goals and orientation of any service program: one based in charity, the other oriented to social change.[4]

Program orientation is often based in a teacher's view of society. Some educators believe that society tends towards equilibrium, with everyone in the proper position. They deem the division of labor a necessary component for a properly functioning economy and think the poor only need opportunity, not power. They do not see social barriers to equality and look for peaceful integration of people into existing structures. Their service-learning programs partner with agencies that cooperate with power holders.[5]

On the other hand, there are educators who see society as divided between dominant and subordinated groups, such as corporations and workers, men and women, and Whites and people of color. They design service-learning programs that work to eliminate injustice through collective action for social change. They organize at the local level with the desire to create a social movement for change. Typically, White, middle-class people, who do not recognize institutional discrimination, tend toward charity programs, and people of color who have suffered institutional discrimination tend toward social-justice service-learning.[6]

The majority of K–16 service-learning programs are charity based and apolitical with a primary focus on student development.[7] Often administration and teachers do not take a justice-oriented stance because they are afraid of losing bipartisan support and funding and do not want to appear to endorse a biased curriculum. Advocates for social change, however, note that universities and communities have a long history of uniting to advocate for justice, as in the civil rights movement, and challenge educators to prepare students to be engaged citizens.[8]

The question remains: What is wrong with charity-based programs? Advocates for social justice critique several aspects of these programs. First, they contend that apolitical education is not possible. Education in general and all service-learning programs in particular are political in that they either support the status quo or work to change it. The decisions surrounding mission, curriculum, methods, and type of reflection all have political dimensions.[9]

We see this more clearly by looking at the concept of service-learning and developing active citizens. Most institutions agree that service-learning is an effective strategy to achieve civic engagement goals,[10] but citizenship means different things to different people. As Kahne, Westheimer, and Rogers suggest, being a good citizen can range from paying taxes and obeying laws, to being active in civic affairs and organizing food drives, to questioning, Why? and working to change the system. Depending on your perspective of what makes a *citizen*, service-learning programs can either support an agenda minimizing the role of government in addressing the needs of the poor, or they can develop a transformative agenda to create more just policies and social practices.[11]

A second area of critique is the missionary ideology of White, privileged students going into areas of poverty to "do for" the poor.[12] Without adequate preparation and knowledge about the populations served, their social and political contexts, and an understanding of discrimination, racism, and classism, students' service experiences often reinforce stereotypes and promote a paternalistic attitude toward those they are serving. Seeing these individual acts of kindness as the "least we can do" cements the notion of being saviors for the poor.

Another potential negative effect is the students' exploitation of those they are helping for their own personal growth and opportunities. I often hear people comment, "It feels good to help the poor," "I get back more than I give," or "Volunteering looks good on a college or job application." While these volunteers are providing a needed service, the motivations are not truly charitable.

A final criticism of charity service programs is that they tend to maintain the status quo of inequity rather than work to create a more just society. When service is seen as an individual act of one person helping another in need, we do not develop the broader perspective of societal inequity, and it limits our ability to address the root causes of injustice.[13]

Having a willingness to help others and devoting time and effort to charity are good, but given the potential for charity-based service-learning programs to reinforce stereotypes, exploit those being served, and impede social change, we should see it as a beginning stage and help students develop a critical stance.

Caring: What Does It Mean to Care?

Care can be interpreted in many different ways. It can mean to help by providing for someone's needs. Likewise, we say care when we mean giving something or someone a great deal of attention to avoid a problem, as in doing something "with great care." Care can invoke the idea of interest or worry, as to be anxious or upset about something, such as, "I care about global warming." We use care to mean providing people or animals with what they need and protecting them, especially where they are young or ill and can't take care of themselves. Care can quite simply mean to like, as in, "I care for Bill," or "I don't care for brussels sprouts." In the expression "to take care of" someone or something, care means to be responsible for him or her or it, and do whatever needs to be done.[14]

How are we using the term caring in the second stage of critical-consciousness development? At the core, it is about the relationship between those providing and those receiving service. We can draw on the work of Nel Noddings and Carol Gilligan to deepen our understanding of what it means to care.

Noddings has written extensively on the ethic of care as it relates to education and society. Her work offers insights into the feelings and connections students should develop in their relationships during service-learning experiences. She describes caring as having regard for someone by giving attention to and having concern for him or her, which includes considering that person's needs and desires. Noddings discusses disposability, derived from the French word disponibilité, meaning investing in someone and making yourself available to that person. Like the expression, "I'm at your disposal," disposability conveys, "I am here for you" and implies, "I care enough to make a commitment."

Engrossment is another concept Noddings uses to express empathy developed from "feeling with" someone. Engrossment involves receiving another person's feelings as your own, rather than simply projecting how you would feel if you were in that person's position. It is a crucial difference in perspective. Rather than putting ourselves in someone else's shoes and intellectually analyzing how we would feel in an objective manner, engrossment involves receiving the person into oneself and actually feeling his or her emotions. In her model, caring involves changing our personal frame of reference in order to feel the other's point of view. The first step in developing this critical awareness is realizing that the situation of the person for whom we are caring could happen to us. This is often a catalyst for action. When we see someone's reality as a possibility for us, we feel compelled to act to remedy the situation.

Noddings believes that relationship is at the center of caring and acknowledges the mutual relationship between the giver and recipient of care. Both the caring and the cared-for contribute to the relationship: care must be received and accepted by the person being helped. The cared-for looks for a sign that the one caring has genuine regard for him or her and is not just providing a routine, meaningless service. Without trust and acceptance in the relationship, the person cared for is dehumanized and feels like an object.[15]

We can easily connect Noddings's theories to effective service-learning practices by examining the role of mutuality and reciprocity in the relationships between service providers, community agencies, and community clients. Service-learners must recognize that while they are contributing a service to the community, they are also benefiting from the experience and taking away important knowledge and personal growth from their interactions. To avoid exploiting those we serve, we must really care, have regard for them, feel with them, and invest ourselves in addressing their needs.

Similarly we find parallels between the stages of critical-consciousness development and Gilligan's research on the stages of moral development. She delineates a progression from *preconventional*, to *conventional*, to *postconventional* based on relationships with an ethic of care. In her initial stage of caring, people are egocentric and make decisions based solely on what is in their best interest and for their own survival. Then, in transitioning to the second stage, individuals recognize their responsibility to others and focus on caring for them, often in a self-sacrificing way that puts the needs of those cared for above their own.

The catalyst to move into the third stage of moral development is recognizing the inequality in the self-sacrificing relationship and realizing that the care giver is also worthy of consideration and care. The focus of the third stage is on the dynamics of the relationship and the interconnection between the other and oneself.[16]

Drawing parallels between Gilligan's theory and how students progress though the stages of critical-consciousness development, we see how students move from charity—"it's mainly about me," to caring—"it's all about them," to social justice—"we need to work together." At the charity stage, students are mainly concerned about themselves, how they feel, and what they get out of the experience. In caring, students begin to develop relationships and consider the needs and feelings of others, and they see it as their responsibility to improve opportunities. At the last stage of social-justice activism, students realize that dismantling an unjust society is in everyone's best interest and requires working in solidarity for our common good.

As a concluding observation, we find an analogous understanding of care by looking at progressive health-care practitioners. Gone is the authoritative, paternalistic health-care-provider-as-expert knows best, declaring what is to occur and demanding passive acceptance. Rather, today's practitioners demonstrate a concern for the well-being of their patients, engaging them as active partners in selecting and meeting their health-care goals. Caring in this therapeutic relationship is "the commitment to alleviate another person's suffering [which] entails the willingness to become personally involved."[17]

Social Justice: What Makes a Person Say, "I can't not do it"?

There are two situations that channel us toward social-justice advocacy. First, when we have a keen awareness of our core values, and are committed to ideals of justice, freedom, and liberty, believe that all people are of equal value, deserving of basic human rights and dignity. We are moved to act on our beliefs when we develop relationships with those we are helping. It is through these relationships that we come to care about individuals and personally invest ourselves in them and their situation. We see their suffering and feel an obligation to do more than provide assistance; we feel it is our responsibility to work for systemic change to end the circumstances of injustice. When we really care, we have to act.

The second situation leading us to a social-justice stance is confronting the contradictions between what we previously thought and the reality we see. Those experiences create a dissonance that forces us to reevaluate our view of reality and what we had known to be true. We need to examine our past biases and faulty assumptions to accommodate the knowledge acquired through service work. We begin to alter our view of others, the world, and ourselves as we come to see how society is based on dominant and subordinate groups and how power and privilege are used to maintain the status quo. This very difficult, often painful experience requires breaking through *hegemony*.

Although hegemony affects everyone, it is not a term familiar to most people. *Hegemony* is the "common sense" understanding of how the world functions and why situations are as they are. To make the concept more tangible, I often think of hegemony as a thick fog or a heavy blanket that covers us, preventing us from seeing reality accurately. Breaking through this barrier is not easy but leads to developing a critical consciousness.

Invisible, yet all-pervasive, hegemonic messages are unconsciously accepted into our minds and regulate our thinking and behavior. Hegemony is so embedded in society and in people's ways of thinking that it projects an accepted view of how the world is, how it has always been, and how it will continue to be.

Hegemony, representing the dominant class's worldview, serves to reinforce the status quo and the power of the privileged class. These ideas are spread through culture, media, and institutions such as schools and churches. The beauty of hegemony is that its messages are so ingrained in the culture that we regularly accept them as our own, even though it is against our best interests. We consent to practices and policies that maintain a society based on injustice and special interests.

A few examples further explain hegemony. If we examine how media, politicians, and ordinary people use language to hide and distort meanings, we can take the first steps toward breaking down myths and stereotypes. At a very young age, we learn that the United States is founded on the ideals of freedom, equality, and justice. These notions are supported by myths such as "racial discrimination is against the law and therefore only exists among a few uneducated people"; "all immigrants can become part of the American melting pot"; and you can "pull yourself up by your bootstraps."

These myths promote the idea that we are all equal and have the same opportunities for social advancement if we simply work hard. The reality is that the playing field is not level, and due to racism, sexism, classism, homophobia, and other institutionalized bias, life is stacked against some and favors others. Stereotypes of people of color, women, and those living in poverty are often reinforced through the home, media, and even school curricula, which provide "common sense" explanations for the differences we see among people and their socioeconomic statuses, such as "boys are better at math than girls," "if they would just learn to speak English . . . ," and "certain people don't want to work."

Breaking through hegemony involves making the invisible visible. In our classrooms we can follow Paulo Freire's path to help students unveil the world of oppression by encouraging them to think critically, engage in critical dialogue, and problematize the reality they see. Why is a particular situation like this? Who benefits? Who is disadvantaged? What are the barriers to change? We should not tell students what to think, but rather enable them to think critically and encourage them to question, challenge, and change reality.

Putting the Pieces Together: Service-Learning, Critical-Consciousness Development, and Social Justice

With an understanding of the elements and stages of critical-consciousness development, we can trace the connection between them through service-learning experiences. As students navigate the road map of critical consciousness, their view of themselves, others, and social issues, and their potential to make change, mature. Table 4.1 presents three portraits of service-learners and maps their transformation as they move through the three stages of critical-consciousness development. While the matrix indicates a directional development, we need to acknowledge that growth does not necessarily occur in a lock-step process. People may be at different levels at the same time and may at times loop back before further advancement. Additionally, since growth is additive, those who have reached the developing stage retain their charitable and caring natures.

"Give a man a fish, and he will eat for a day. Teach a man to fish, and he will eat for the rest of his life." This common proverb provides an image for the charity and caring stages of critical-consciousness development through service-learning; but to complete the metaphor we need include the social-change aspect and make room at the river for all to fish.

Ethic of Service: Why Do I Serve? How Do I View Service Work?

As individuals become more critically aware, their ethic of service moves from charity to caring to social justice. These changes are seen in their orientation to service and their motivation to serve, as well as in awareness of the reciprocal nature of service-learning. In the initial stage, students' orientation to service is based on charity, and they are motivated to give back to the community because they have so much, but also because helping others

Table 4.1. Stages of White Critical-Consciousness Development and Service-Learning

		Initial: Charity	Emerging: Caring	Developing: Social Justice
Ethic of Service	**Metaphor**	Give a fish.	Teach to fish.	Make room at the river for all to fish.
	Service orientation	Charity: give back to community Do for others.	Caring: compassion & empathy Do for, but are in relationship with, others.	Social justice: systemic change, work in solidarity Do with others.
	Motivation to serve	"Helping others feels good." "I learn a lot." "A great opportunity."	"I can make a difference." "Sense of efficacy & agency"	"My liberation is connected to yours." "I can't not act."
	Reciprocity in service	"I get back more than I give."	"I receive & contribute."	"We work together for common good."
Awareness of Self & Others	**White racial-identity formation**	Color-blindness Do not see their own race. "I don't see race."	Awareness of racism, but don't know what to do Often feel guilt & frustration.	Potential to be White antiracist allies to people of color Begin to unlearn internalized racism.
	Diversity	Everyone is the same or everyone has differences.	Acknowledge differences, value diversity.	Interconnectedness: diversity within inclusiveness.

(continued)

Table 4.1. (continued)

		Initial: Charity	Emerging: Caring	Developing: Social Justice
Awareness of Self & Others	**View of the other**	Deficit view of others: "less fortunate, disadvantaged" *Stereotypical: some deserve help, others don't.*	View others as individuals, each with own story, not stereotype *Realize "it could be me."*	View others as equals: community members seen as strengths & resources *Are connected to others.*
	Reflection on self & otherness	Unaware of self in relation to otherness *Think everyone is basically the same.*	Compare others' lives to theirs *Begin to question beliefs, attitudes, & what has previously been taught/learned.*	Critical reflection on assumptions, privilege, oppression, power structures surrounding race, class, gender, etc.
Awareness of Social Issues	**View of the world**	World is simple & basically good. *Some people need help due to dysfunctional families, poverty, or poor education.*	World is bigger & more complex than thought. *See inequity & contradictions between societal stated beliefs & reality.*	Injustice is inherent in social, economic & political systems on a global level.
	Source of the problem	Individual responsibility: "if everyone just tried harder" "Pull oneself up by the bootstraps." *Blame the victim.*	The need for government to protect & ensure basic rights for all *Avoid judging others for situations out of their control.*	Policies & practices maintain & reproduce the status quo that favors certain groups at the expense of others.
	View of social justice	Increase resources.	Treat people fairly & increase their opportunities.	Examine root causes of injustice & work for systemic change.

in need makes them feel good about themselves. Describing this win-win situation, students often state they "get back more than [they] give." In this stance they are "doing for" others.

As students emerge into critical consciousness, their orientation to service becomes one of caring. As a result of seeing injustice, they develop empathy and compassion for the people they are helping and feel morally obligated to ease their suffering. As a result of past service experiences, students gain a sense of efficacy and agency and are motivated to serve because they know what they do matters. They become aware of the reciprocal relationship between those providing and receiving service, acknowledging what they are gaining in terms of knowledge, perspective, and personal growth. At this stage, service providers are still "doing for" others, but the difference is that they are in relationship with those they are helping.

The orientation of service at the developing level is one of social transformation for equity and justice. White, privileged individuals come to realize that both the powerful and the powerless are dehumanized when oppression and injustice are allowed to continue. They see the connection between their liberation and that of subordinated groups and commit to work in solidarity with them. Individuals in the developing stage feel morally obligated to make the world more just and work as allies with oppressed groups for the common good. They "do with" others.

Awareness of Self and Others: "What's race got to do with it?"

Gaining a greater awareness of self is so inseparable from having a broader perspective of others that we need to discuss these elements of critical-consciousness development together. The number one task of White people in this country is to understand the social construction of race and the role that race, racism, and White privilege has played in history and continues to play today. As we grow in this understanding, we develop more accurate views of others, the world, and ourselves. As students move from charity to caring to social justice, they develop a greater understanding of identity formation and diversity.

Students at the initial level of critical consciousness are unaware of race. We often hear them say they are color-blind and "don't see race." In addition to not seeing others' race, they are unaware of their own Whiteness, because color blindness is an expression of White privilege. Uninformed about historical and current social inequalities, students believe that discrimination no longer exists and that we are all the same or we all have differences. At this stage, service providers hold a deficit view of those they are serving, referring to them as less fortunate and disadvantaged. Their view of others is stereotypical, and they believe some people are deserving of help, and others are not. They are unaware of themselves in relation to otherness and believe everyone is basically the same.

Students with an emerging critical consciousness see difference and value diversity. Usually as a result of relationships with people of color, they become aware of racism, but do not know what to do about it and often experience discomfort, shame, guilt, and anger. Their service activities enable them to see those they are helping as individuals, and poverty statistics become real and meaningful. Students compare their own situation with that of those living in poverty, and realize the role of chance in determining one's situation. In the event of unemployment, illness, or family change, many of us could easily find ourselves without money for basic needs. New perspectives and understandings compel students to question previously held notions and beliefs about others and critique what they have been taught as truth.

As individuals reach the developing social-justice stage of critical consciousness, they see their potential to be White antiracists and to work as allies of people of color in fighting injustice. The first task is acknowledging internalized racism and beginning to unlearn racist ways of thinking and being. Through relationships with others and personal reflection, they appreciate the interconnectedness of humanity and create spaces that support diversity within an inclusive environment.

These students view all people with dignity, seeing them as worthy of love and deserving of basic human rights. Their view of others changes from deficiency to one of strength, seeing community members of oppressed groups as strengths and resources for addressing social injustices. Critical reflection leads them to continually question their assumptions and privilege and reveals power structures that perpetuate discrimination against oppressed groups based on race, class, gender, sexual orientation, level of education, and other biases.

Awareness of Social Issues: What's Really Going On Here?

Gaining a greater awareness of social issues involves having an accurate view of the world, understanding the sources of contemporary problems, and considering how best to solve them. To students in the initial stage of consciousness, the world is basically good and full of hope for all who want to take advantage of opportunities. Social and economic advancement is based on merit, which means all those who work hard can pull themselves up by their bootstraps. They understand that some people need help, but think it is usually due to a dysfunctional family, poverty, or poor education. The answer to economic and social problems is to increase resources through donations, collections, and drives. In charity-based service programs, students receive long-term benefits in terms of personal growth and academic achievement.

Caring moves service-learners into the emerging stage of critical consciousness. As they reflect on the injustices they see around them and the contradictions between societal beliefs and principles and lived experiences, they realize the world is bigger and more complex than they had thought. Students question the government's role in protecting and ensuring basic human rights for all. They avoid judging others for situations over which they have no control. Their view of social justice is treating people fairly, and they work to increase opportunities for those in need.

Service activities at the emerging stage involve working in soup kitchens, homeless shelters, and food shelves. Students also work at drop-in centers, posttreatment housing projects, and schools serving students who live in poverty and/or come from immigrant populations. Other marginalized populations served are the elderly and those living with mental or physical challenges.

Students at the developing stage of critical consciousness recognize that injustice is inherent in social, economic, and political systems on a global level. The sources of injustice are governmental and corporate policies and educational practices that support and reproduce the status quo, favoring privileged groups at the expense of others. As a result, they seek social justice by examining the root causes of injustice and working for systemic change. Service work at this level can no longer be described as "projects" or "activities" because of the ongoing, sustained level of commitment required. Such work includes advocacy for groups who cannot advocate for themselves, such as children and immigrants; coalition building; public education on political, economic, and social issues; and work with grassroots organizations to advance social and environmental causes.

Conclusion

Mainstream service-learning programs are primarily located at the initial stage of critical consciousness. Individuals are immersed in society's hegemonic messages and, as a result, do not question underlying assumptions and biases. Living in segregated communities limits contact with diverse populations; and, with few opportunities to build relationships across racial, ethnic, and class divisions, students receive their information from both overt and covert messages in media and from individuals who surround them. This results in faulty opinions and judgments based on inaccurate and often prejudicial information, which reinforces racism, classism, sexism, and a naive worldview.

High-school and college service programs that are committed to social justice are most often located at the emerging stage. As a result of volunteering at agencies serving people living in poverty and other marginalized populations, individuals at this level begin to think critically about previously held notions of race, class, and gender. Their service work creates spaces for direct interaction with diverse populations, dispelling previously held prejudices and initiating a new understanding of "us" and "them." Research, accurate information, and class discussion are tools that reinforce moral and civic values, a desire to alleviate suffering, and the development of skills to effect change. Formerly isolated and insulated from reality, students leave their suburban bubble and get out of their comfort zone, gaining new perspectives on others and the world.

Entering into the developing stage of critical consciousness requires a change of minds and hearts at the most fundamental level. Once individuals become aware of how the system awards certain groups of people access to power and the ability to define reality, they undergo a total reordering of what they believe to be true. Growing more aware of power relations, individuals are awakened to the hidden hegemonic messages that form people's consciousness, political opinions, knowledge of self and others, and worldview, and that manipulate their actions in the interests of the dominant group, rather than in their own interests.

For members of the White middle and upper-middle classes, developing a critical consciousness forces them to acknowledge their White (and, if applicable, male) privilege and reflect on how their actions and attitudes contribute to or work against maintaining the status quo. On a personal level, they need to confront their willingness to give up power, so that others can take a seat at the table.

Humbled in their new awareness, individuals at this level move from knowing the answers to asking questions, from being in charge to being an ally, and from concerns of individual suffering to working for systemic change. Arriving at the developing stage of consciousness is a result of hard work, critical reflection with others striving for integrity, and studying the operations of political and economic systems. Being at this level puts individuals in a difficult, and at times painful, position because once awakened, they cannot return to a simpler, naive existence of not knowing. Well-designed service-learning programs support students as they see possibilities for change and decide to live with integrity and work for social justice.

CHAPTER FIVE

Navigating the Stages of Critical-Consciousness Development

Equipped with a good understanding of critical-consciousness elements and the developmental stages that students experience as they become more critically aware, our questions become, How can educators help students navigate through the stages of critical-consciousness development? and How do students move from here to there? The short answer is through information, experiences, and reflection. Table 5.1, "Navigating the Stages of White Critical-Consciousness Development," provides an overview by highlighting information, experiences, and reflection for navigating from one stage to another.

It is vitally important that student activities be stage appropriate to prepare them for the next steps. Taking a lesson from early practices in diversity training, how often have multicultural education efforts been thwarted by well-meaning workshop leaders presenting internalized racism and White privilege to White audiences who were unaware of their own race? We need to take students at their starting point and intentionally design curricula, experiences, and reflection activities that respectfully point them on their journey of self-discovery, discovery of others, and appreciation of the world.

The guidelines presented in this chapter offer educators a framework to promote student growth. It is not necessarily all-inclusive nor the sole path for stage navigation. While we may imagine the movement to be one-directional, students often need to travel back and reinforce foundational pieces during their journey because of the dynamic nature of student learning and development.

Table 5.1. Navigating the Stages of White Critical-Consciousness Development

	Initial *From charity* *to caring*	*Emerging* *From caring to* *social justice*	*Developing* *Maturing* *one's critical* *consciousness*
Information & research	Population served & related social issues, such as homelessness & poverty	History of race & racism, systems of oppressions, institutional racism; research own racial & ethnic history	Political & economic systems, capitalism & globalization, critical theory
Service experiences	Direct service to people & agencies dealing with poverty; interactions with people from other ethnic & racial groups	Agencies & organizations addressing both immediate needs & long-term solutions	Advocacy & grassroots community groups, lobbying & political organizations
Reflection: inward	Reflection on personal values, responsibility to others	Reflection on White racial identity & privilege; internalized racism, sexism, & classism, etc.	Reflection on power, knowledge & control; hegemony, counterhegemonic practices, collective action
Reflection: outward	Reflection on how things are & how they should be; create alternative vision for society	Reflection on systems of oppression & institutional racism	Reflection on power relations, class structure & social reproduction; cultural capital, discipline & surveillance
Reflection: methods	Reflection through discussion, perspective taking, problem posing, films	Reflection through critical dialogue, perspective taking, problem posing, critical narratives	Reflection through critical dialogue, ideological critique, & discourse analysis

Moving from Charity to Caring

Students at the initial stage of critical-consciousness development need accurate information, experiences that provoke questions, and reflection on their values and worldview. Students who have had limited contact with diverse populations often receive stereotypical, incomplete, and/or flawed information from institutions, media, and family, leaving them ill-equipped to understand current social issues.

Before students engage in service experiences, they need to become knowledgeable about the population they are serving and the issues it faces. For example, students who are serving food at a homeless shelter should research poverty and homelessness. By conducting their own research, rather than being told in lecture format, they discover for themselves the characteristics of the average person without housing, the hourly wage required for a livable income, and the availability and rates for affordable housing in the area. If students are working with immigrant populations, they should investigate United States immigration history and hear stories of current immigrants, to better understand this complex issue and make it personal.

Service experiences at this stage should include direct work with marginalized groups of people, such as individuals living in poverty, individuals from other ethnic or racial groups, or individuals with mental or physical challenges. When students interact with these clients and with agency volunteers, they create a connection to others and increase their understanding of diverse groups and their situations. Students also develop empathy and become more compassionate when they see humanity in others and begin to understand their struggles and suffering.

Equipped with accurate information and new perspectives from service experiences, students have a foundation on which they can build a deeper awareness of themselves, others, and social issues through reflection. In moving from the initial to the emerging stage of critical consciousness, students need time to reflect on their values and their responsibilities. Discussion of topics such as human dignity, equality, basic human rights, and justice provides them with opportunities to state, refine, and clarify what they believe and to connect how their service experiences helped clarify their values and beliefs.

Students also need opportunities to reflect on their worldview, analyzing how things are and imagining how they could be. Reflection and discussion on their service experiences uncover questions of inequities and contradictions between stated beliefs and the lived realities of many people, laying the groundwork for examining beliefs, assumptions, and bias. Reflection that progresses from students' values and responsibilities to the gap between how things are and how they should be, and that examines the emotional connection to others, has the potential to increase students' critical consciousness.

Our role as teachers is to assist students as they develop a more critical awareness by creating activities and experiences that provoke reflection and foster growth. Education for democracy and justice accepts students where they are, gives them input and opportunities to utilize critical thinking, and allows them to actively engage in constructing their own new knowledge. We educators must be deliberate in our design to avoid practices in which students are manipulated into uncritically accepting our views or become defensive and resistant to perceived manipulation.

A method to dispel potential feelings of coercion is using a "third medium" as stimulus for reflection. If we consider the student and the teacher as two mediums in the classroom, then by introducing a third medium, such as role-playing, film, community members, or service experiences, we put students at the center of the learning process, and the teacher's role is to facilitate discussion. Students can begin to question their assumptions, think critically, and form an accurate view of the present world as well as the world they want to create. Then they can begin to create it. Stage-appropriate methods of reflection include discussion, perspective taking, problem posing, and role-playing. Films, narratives, and student journals can be powerful sources to stimulate growth.

Moving from Caring to Social Justice

The work at the emerging level for White people is to develop their racial identity, become aware of White privilege, and understand oppression and institutional racism. Developing a critical consciousness at the emerging stage requires continued experiences with otherness, but also introspection at a fundamental level to confront internalized racism. Students need to examine our nation's history and legacy of racism and how White people have benefited—and continue to benefit—from racist policies and practices.

To move from the emerging to developing stage of critical consciousness, students need information on systems of oppression by researching the "isms," that is, racism, sexism, classism, ableism, ageism, and heterosexism, and how they intersect in a system of domination. Students can also advance in their knowledge of others by seeking information on the contributions, challenges, and oppression of Native Americans, African Americans, Asian-Pacific Americans, and Latinos, and by studying the history of nativism and racial discrimination in the United States and its role in the social construction of race.

In addition to learning about and from individuals from these representative groups, students investigate their own racial and ethnic group in order to identify their history. Students must develop a positive view of Whiteness and see their potential to use their privilege to create a more just world. Educators can affirm students' White identity by presenting examples of White people who have worked in alliance with people of color to fight inequity throughout history, as well as those who continue the struggle today.[1]

In developing critical consciousness, individuals should engage in service experiences with agencies that serve marginalized groups and that are not merely addressing immediate needs, but are working toward social justice and long-term solutions. Participating in long-term projects increases students' sense of agency and contributes to their identity formation as morally and civically engaged community members. Working with these agencies provides role models for social justice and demonstrates the power of working collectively.

To promote growth at this stage, teachers must be adept at creating reflection activities that are both effective and sensitive. As White students gain awareness of their racial identity, internalized racism, and White privilege, teachers should anticipate the range of emotions students are feeling and support them on their journey. Inward-reflection activities assist students in developing a positive self-definition of their race. The aim is to begin where students are in their racial identity formation and support them as they navigate the phases of White racial identity.[2]

Obviously, racial-identity formation requires significant time, effort, and experience, and this is one of the reasons most service-learners do not achieve a critical consciousness at the developing stage until late college or adulthood, if at all. Asking provocative questions such as, do your actions contribute to or struggle against oppression? or how are both the oppressor and the oppressed dehumanized by acts of oppression? can provoke students to action.

Outward reflection can move students' belief that racism equals individual acts of prejudice to an understanding of the institutionalized nature of racism—how it is embedded in policies and practices that have discriminated, and continue to discriminate, against subordinated groups in our society. Media critique, racial profiling, prison statistics, and high-school drop-out rates are all topics for reflection, discussion, and critical dialogue that contribute to students' ability to see institutional racism.

In addition to critical reflection on race, students begin to deconstruct language and myths, examining how media, politicians, and ordinary people use language to conceal and contrive meanings. For decades, people have used coded words to hide racist or sexist attitudes and devalue racial, ethnic, and gender identities.[3] For example, people often use the term *urban* when they mean schools with high percentages of students of color and/or high poverty levels. Other expressions include "welfare queen," "articulate person of color," and women who are "aggressive" rather than *assertive* or "emotional" rather than *compassionate*. Understanding the meaning behind the words is a powerful step in the deconstruction of hegemony. Likewise, exploding myths, such as the *meritocracy, the American melting pot, and pulling oneself up by the bootstraps* increases students' ability to see reality.

Once students reconnect with earlier reflections on their values, moral obligation, and vision of a more just world; reaffirm their developing ethic of service and sense of efficacy and agency; and integrate a clearer understanding of oppression, racialized identities, and institutionalized discrimination, they can commit themselves to struggle against all forms of oppression. As they enter into the developing stage, they continue their interrogations of self and of hegemonic messages and build coalitions that work for social justice. In addition to methods of reflection cited in the last stage of discussion (perspective taking, problem posing, and role-playing), emerging stage-appropriate strategies include critical dialogue, content analysis for myth busting, and language deconstruction. Films, critical narratives, speakers, and student-conducted research through surveys and interviews are powerful sources to stimulate growth.

Maturing One's Critical Consciousness

As individuals enter into the developing stage of critical consciousness, becoming more aware of self, others, and the world is more vital and intense. People at this stage need to understand the connection between power and knowledge and recognize how power is used in coercive ways to control society and control individuals in body, mind, and spirit.

In order to critique the system and find opportunities to challenge, reform, or dismantle it, individuals need information on the history and current operations of political and economic systems. A foundation in critical theory is necessary for individuals striving for social transformation. Reading works of Apple, Bourdieu, Foucault, and Giroux provides a framework for critically understanding knowledge, truth, power, and control. Paulo Freire and Myles

Horton are sources for implementing critical pedagogy with community workers and connecting liberation and theology in education. Ira Shor, Henry Giroux, and Peter McLaren provide visions and prospects of critical pedagogy in high-school and university settings. It is essential to develop skills in critical thinking, the evaluation of traditional and electronic information sources, and communication.[4]

At the developing stage, service experiences that advance volunteers in their skills and awareness tend to be with advocacy organizations, grassroots community alliances, and lobbying and political-action groups. White people with a high level of critical consciousness work as allies in solidarity with marginalized groups for social justice and mutual liberation. They work collaboratively to find spaces that penetrate hegemony and challenge the status quo.

Inward reflection at the developing level necessitates deep introspection about one's concept of knowledge and truth and continual inquiry into the questions, why do I think X? and who benefits from my thinking and acting in a particular way? Reflection on how to connect the individual act with collective movements and the personal with the political augment the potential for transformative change. Individuals constantly question themselves and society by critically reflecting on how assumptions and bias regarding race, class, and gender impact thoughts, decisions, and events. Deepening the understanding of hegemony and finding ways to counteract it are strategies leading to collective praxis.

Outward reflection engenders a critical investigation into the strengths and weaknesses of democracy and capitalism and the effect of capitalism's collision with democracy, as well as the impact of globalization on national sovereignty. Increasing one's awareness of class structure, exploitation, and social reproduction requires information and critical reflection. Other topics for reflection include culture and cultural capital: how it is formed and reproduced in our society, by whom and for what purpose, and the role of media in forming perceptions. Being critically aware also requires an understanding of the arbitrary nature of knowledge; the regimes of truth that dictate what is true, normal, and acceptable; and power in the form of surveillance and self-discipline that regulate our behavior. Unveiling these hidden ideologies and practices is a component of critical reflection.

Inward and outward critical reflection at the developing level also includes opportunities to envision systemic change for social justice. Recognizing the power of collective thought and critical dialogue, informed citizens can problematize reality, articulate the issues, and commit to a new social order of justice. Collective reflecting, finding spaces for contestations, and acting result in a powerful praxis that attacks the root causes of injustice and creates transformative change.

Reflection topics at this level are complex and are addressed repeatedly in a never-ending attempt to know reality in oneself, others, and the world. Methods for critical reflection include critical dialogue to challenge and support each other in development, ideological critique to reveal power relations, and discourse analysis to unravel the constructed meanings of knowledge and practices.

Conclusion

How do we help students navigate the stages of critical-consciousness development through service-learning? As I stated in the beginning of the chapter, the simple answer is "information, experiences, and reflection." This model provides a framework from which to begin by taking students where they are and creating learning experiences that promote growth. While looking at the information and activities in the developing stage, where individuals are maturing in their critical consciousness, can seem like an overwhelming, daunting task—as the Horton and Freire book title *We Make the Road by Walking*[5] reminds us—we should take the first step and keep going. Lisa Lenhart-Murphy, service-learning coordinator and trainer, advises teachers and administrators initiating projects and programs: "Build on what you have, start small, and make it good. Take baby steps, but keep on walking."

My intent in these first five chapters has been to provide you with an understanding of how individuals develop a critical consciousness and a social-justice orientation to service work. This three-part social-justice model for service-learning is a road map to guide educators in building service programs that are robust enough to develop critical awareness and a moral and civic commitment for social justice in their students. The road map identifies four essential elements that lead to critical-consciousness development; three stages of White critical-conscious development; and stage-appropriate information, experiences, and reflection that are needed in order to navigate through the stages.

The second part of the book offers new insights on stage-appropriate information, experiences, and reflection that advance students in their knowledge, understanding, and commitment in a respectful, supportive manner. It also provides concrete examples, ideas, and resources to both improve practice and increase long-term participation in community action to create a more equitable, just society for all.

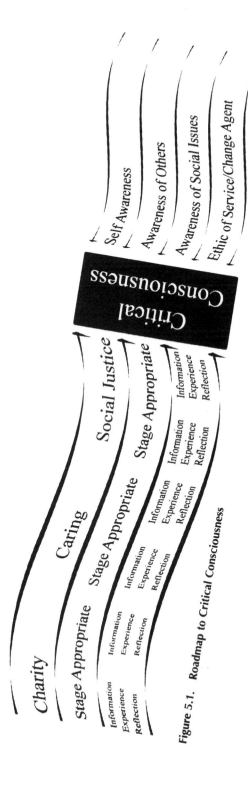

Charity

Stage Appropriate

Caring

Stage Appropriate

Social Justice

Stage Appropriate

Information
Experience
Reflection

Information
Experience
Reflection

Information
Experience
Reflection

Information
Experience
Reflection

Critical
Consciousness

Self Awareness

Awareness of Others

Awareness of Social Issues

Ethic of Service/Change Agent

Figure 5.1. Roadmap to Critical Consciousness

PART II

ENGAGING STUDENTS IN SOCIAL CHANGE THROUGH SERVICE-LEARNING

CHAPTER SIX

K–12 Education: Strategies for Effective Service-Learning Practices

While the journey ahead can be difficult, it is important to remember that we are not alone. Many thoughtful educators have been working with these issues for years, and they provide insight and instruction as we embark, with purpose, to transform our educational practices.

Incorporating Research-Based Strategies in Secondary Schools

In *Unpacking What Works in Service-Learning*, Shelley Billig synthesizes several years of research as well as recent studies to present research-based practices that improve student outcomes.[1] Research findings from multiple studies support eight practices that can increase the impact of your service-learning program. These practices form the foundation for the K–12 Service-Learning Standards for Quality Practices. Noting that the impact of service-learning depends on implementation, each section in this chapter begins with a short summary of the research results presented in Billig's article, then describes ways to incorporate them into a service-learning program.

Curriculum Integration
Research shows that student achievement can be significantly increased when service is integrated into the subject matter and a clear connection exists between goals and activities. Curriculum integration requires developing an academic unit with clearly stated learning objectives, lesson plans for

activities that engage students in achieving the goals, and an assessment plan that measures student outcomes.[2]

A key element in developing effective service-learning projects is making the curricular connection. We have all seen service projects in which much effort is put into implementation and, while it met a community need, the connection to the curriculum was vague, and learning outcomes were weak. What follows is an overview of some basic elements in curriculum development and steps to ensure curriculum integration.

There are two approaches to service-learning curriculum development. One path maps objectives beginning with the course. This is useful when the service context is an individual course, a specific department, or a subject area at a grade level. For example, in the world-language department, our objective was to gain a better understanding of globalization and its economic and social effects in Latin America. With that object in mind, we prepared a course of study that examined sweatshops, and students designed a plan to have the board of directors adopt a policy of a sweat-free school.

The second path starts with the project and maps objectives back to the curriculum. Perhaps your students are already involved in food drives, collections, or tutoring programs, which provide great service but are not directly tied to academic learning. With these projects in mind, you would build learning objectives and instruction that deepen the service experience and student learning.

For example, a parent of a junior-high student who had ties to an orphanage in North Korea wanted students to help raise funds for the orphans. Working with the service-learning coordinator, they created a curriculum introducing the students to the history, context, and situation of North Korea in general and the orphanage specifically. The students were invited to be in solidarity with the orphans by giving up luxury items (soda, CDs, movie tickets, or something similar) and donating the money to the fund drive. As a result of the academic tie-in, three hundred students contributed $1,500 in five days.

The process is similar with both approaches. The challenge is to critically reexamine the process as well as the content of how we decide what to teach. Responding to the following three questions builds the framework for making the academic connection to the service:

What do you want the students to learn? This is your objective or learning outcome. Formulating your educational objectives and outcomes is the foundation of your unit design, lesson plans, and assessments. You need to understand and explain to the students what you want them to learn and why it is important. Objectives can encompass cognitive outcomes of academic knowledge and thinking skills, affective outcomes related to attitudinal changes and values clarification, and behavioral outcomes that result in action.

How will this be accomplished? These are your lesson plans, class activities, and assignments. To fully answer this question, think through the progression of teaching and learning, step by step. Some elements of good lesson design include activities in which students are actively engaged, use critical thinking skills, and have choice. Using a third medium such as invited speakers, films, music, readings, student presentations, or role-playing creates variety and provides students with a broad range of input.

How do you measure student learning? This is your assessment and grading plan. Although assessment and grading are two different concepts, creating a rubric that sets your expectations, assesses student learning, and translates performance into a grade incorporates both tasks. When students know your expectations and assessment plan before beginning the unit, it increases their levels of performance and success. Assessment can include formal and informal measurements, checklists for performance, traditional quizzes and tests, projects, presentations, student self-evaluation, and reflection activities.

Addressing these questions becomes deliberate if teachers know where the students are in terms of critical-consciousness development. Using the social-justice model for service-learning, we can examine the four essential elements (self-awareness, awareness of others, awareness of social issues, and seeing potential to make change), as well as the three stages of critical-consciousness development (charity, caring, and social justice), to determine the appropriate outcomes and curricular objectives.

Ongoing Cognitively Challenging Reflection Activities
Research shows that reflection improves the quality of student learning and strengthens the long-term impact of service-learning experiences. To maximize results, reflection should be ongoing and challenging, and include a variety of methods and formats.[3]

After connecting the service component to the curriculum, the second most important factor in developing an effective service-learning program is embedding reflection into the unit, by creating opportunities for critical reflection before, during, and after the project. *Reflection* consists of using critical-thinking skills to prepare for and learn from a service experience.

You should allot class time for discussions and reflection activities and design assignments that help students reflect on activities both subjectively and objectively. This develops the use of higher-order thinking skills and increases the students' awareness of how and what they learn.

The types of reflection activities and their functions will differ, depending on when they occur and the developmental stage of students' critical consciousness. Reflection before service helps teachers and students prepare. Activities assess student awareness of the social issue and the people they are helping. These reflections connect to previous experiences, help uncover common misconceptions, or illustrate the impact of different perspectives. Preservice reflection clarifies values and beliefs and instigates discussions about contradictions between what we say we value and reality. It helps us assess the knowledge and skills we already possess or identify those we lack, in order to adequately prepare for service.

Reflection during service supports students by providing opportunities to share feelings, successes, and concerns; identify and discuss challenges and problems; and analyze the complexities and contexts of the social issue. Reflection activities also help students articulate what and how they are learning.

As the service experience draws to a close, reflection activities continue to assess student learning and project outcomes, as well as looking forward to additional student commitments or goals that address this or other community needs.

Varying the methods of reflection and raising the level of challenge of reflection activities are two factors that increase student learning and long-term impact. In an effort to reach all students, the methods of reflection can include reading, writing, speaking, listening, and sometimes even just being still and thinking. They may include visual arts, music, drama, role-playing, simulations, and film. Other ideas are small- and large-group discussions, individual or small-group meetings between student(s) and teacher, journaling, class presentations, poster presentations, pictorial essays, responding to guided questions, letters to oneself, poetry, and scrapbooks.

To challenge students in their thinking, teachers pose questions that emphasize different learning styles. Silver, Strong, and Perini describe four types of questions in *The Strategic Teacher*:

1. Mastery questions emphasize recalling information (summarize, prioritize, remember).
2. Understanding questions emphasize analysis and use of evidence (compare and contrast, hypothesize, disprove this statement).

3. Interpersonal questions emphasize feelings, values, and personal experiences (about which issue do you feel strongest, preferences, and how would you feel /react if . . .).

4. Self-expression questions emphasize imagination (create metaphors, design a symbol, what if . . . ? and suppose and imagine the effect if one thing changed).[4]

Jim Toole, founder of Compass Institute, creates a hierarchy of questions for reflection using *Bloom's Taxonomy*, challenging student thinking at higher cognitive levels. Lisa Lenhart-Murphy, service-learning coordinator at Benilde-St. Margaret's School, adapted his framework for volunteering at a homeless shelter:

- Knowledge: What were your first impressions of the shelter?
- Comprehension: How was this shelter similar or different from what you expected?
- Application: How has volunteering at the shelter changed your perception of the homeless?
- Analysis: What parts of the experience have been most challenging to you?
- Synthesis: What have you personally learned about yourself from this service?
- Evaluation: What ideas do you have to help the situation of homelessness?[5]

Refer to Table 5.1, "Navigating the Stages of White Critical-Consciousness Development," to select the appropriate reflection methods and activities. This gives ideas for stage-appropriate topics and methods for student reflection on awareness of self, others, and social issues.

Youth Voice

Research shows that when students take leadership in planning and directing service-learning experiences, academic and civic engagement increases. Similarly, when they are given opportunities to voice their opinions and make presentations, students' public-speaking and leadership skills improve, as they begin to see their role as change-agents.[6]

Educators often attempt to include student voice by asking students to join a board or steering committee, which can be effective if done well, but more often results in students attending boring meetings where little is accomplished and their opinions are minimized. However, when we convince students that we want and value their opinions, their voice comes through loud and clear. When young people have meaningful tasks and decision-making ability, youth voice becomes authentic. Students who have leadership opportunities increase their sense of efficacy and agency, fostering two of the essential elements of critical-consciousness development: deeper awareness of self and seeing one's potential to make change.

Youth voice can be cultivated in two arenas: in the classroom and with outside audiences. In the classroom, students can take the lead in planning, implementing, and assessing the service-learning experience. This involves investigating community needs, making contacts with community agencies, completing school forms such as permission slips and bus requests, and discussing and agreeing on learning objectives, reflection activities, and assessment. How do students develop these skills? One method is for the teacher to provide a framework, outlining necessary decisions and asking students questions that help organize their deliberations.

If students jump to a faulty conclusion or an undoable plan, teachers help them redirect the plan by problem posing:

- "What would happen if . . . ?"
- "Are there different actions that would . . . ?"
- "Can you anticipate any problems with . . . ?"

Sometimes even well-conceived plans fail, for a variety of reasons, providing an opportunity for evaluation and adaptation. For example, a group of junior-high science students researched and planned a campaign to alert neighborhood residents to the environmental damage yard fertilizers were causing in area lakes. They wanted to stencil sewer covers as reminders. When the city rejected the students' proposal, they adjusted the plan by designing and distributing brochures to the community.

Another way to develop student leadership is by engaging older students as mentors. In addition to giving the older students leadership roles, mentored students learn about leadership skills through observation. This method is built on the medical model of "see one, do one, teach one"; students learn by doing and teaching. Service clubs can be organized in pods, with older students as pod leaders for younger students. At meetings they take attendance, lead reflection activities, and organize and document service activities.

Presenting to real audiences is the second arena in which youth voice can find expression. From identifying community issues to presenting proposals and reporting results, students can really shine at board meetings, city-council sessions, state committee meetings, and educational conferences. Not only do they gain invaluable experiences and increased confidence, they are a welcome feature on the agenda and can often be more effective than adults in achieving their goal with a particular audience.

Respect for Diversity

Research shows that student outcomes in civic engagement and character development are enhanced when teachers explicitly discuss diversity and talk about respect, equity, prejudice, and discrimination. Students must explore their own identities and the meaning of democracy.[7] Teachers should be clear about their expectations and model a caring attitude for all.

When people hear the word *diversity*, racial diversity is the usually the first concept that comes to mind. Given our nation's history of racism and discriminatory practices and their enduring effect on society, it is important to talk about race, while recognizing that diversity encompasses much more. Diversity includes a myriad of categories: racial, ethnic, cultural, language, gender, and class diversity, as well as diversity in the areas of sexual orientation, ability, appearance, age, religion, and learning style, and diversity related to experiences, ideas, beliefs, and attitudes. It is also important to acknowledge the wide diversity within any particular group and the similarities across groups.

Teachers must be aware of their students' knowledge, experiences, and attitudes about people from other ethnic, racial, and social backgrounds when they prepare discussions on race and racism. By determining their location in the stages of critical-consciousness development, teachers can create stage-appropriate lessons, which scaffold the information, experiences, and reflection activities to promote student growth and minimize negative reactions of resistance, denial, and defensiveness.

Teachers begin the diversity conversation by asking students to write down how they identify or describe themselves, which is followed by discussion about the types of markers they have mentioned. It is common that people often do not mention a dominant characteristic because that is seen as "normal" and therefore not distinct or distinguishing. The discussion can be furthered by asking students to list as many "-isms" as they can, and following this up by introducing the concepts of power, dominant and subordinate groups, and agents and targets of discrimination/oppression. A concluding discussion can expand the idea that we all have many aspects to our identities. In some aspects we may be in the dominant group, with the power to be either an agent of oppression or an ally working to dismantle an oppressive system. In other aspects, we belong to subordinated groups and are at risk of being targets of discrimination.

In preparing for service-learning experiences, an important first step is to learn about clients and their situations, building an understanding of and empathy for them. In many sites, students work with clients who have different backgrounds and experiences, and students need to be informed. My goal is for students to break down stereotypes and misinformation and come to appreciate that everyone has a story, is doing the best he or she can at this moment, and is deserving of dignity and care; misfortune can befall anyone. This follows a three-step process.

First, have students reflect on and discuss their beliefs, values, and responsibilities. It is helpful to draw upon readings and well-known, accepted documents such as the Declaration of Independence, the U.S. Constitution and Bill of Rights, the United Nations Universal Declaration of Human Rights, and other United Nations documents such as the International Covenant on Economic, Social, and Cultural Rights, and the Convention on the Rights of the Child.

Second, ask students to list what people say or think about the population group (not necessarily what they believe, but what they have heard). For example, immigrants and nondocumented workers "take our jobs, do not pay taxes, and come to get welfare money." This helps to put commonly held attitudes on the table without fear of accusation.

Third, gather facts through Internet searches, interactive online quizzes, guest speakers, films, or readings. This process dispels myths and stereotypes, replaces misconceptions with accurate information, and empowers students with knowledge.

The teacher has two additional responsibilities regarding student attitudes and perspectives. First, ensure that students are well prepared and capable of appropriate and caring behavior in relationships with clients. People served may be vulnerable and disenfranchised individuals, such as children, developmentally challenged adults, and the elderly, and our rule is, "First, do no harm." Second, we help students be humble in their approach, realizing that they are not just giving their time and help to others, they are also benefiting and taking from those they are serving by gaining knowledge, skills, understandings, and broader perspectives.

Meaningful Service
Research shows that when students feel they are providing meaningful service, there are greater outcomes in learning, skill building, and engagement. Qualities of "meaningful service" include work that is interesting and relevant to students, that is useful and meets an important need, and that is challenging but not overwhelming. When students choose the issue that they will address, have a personal connection, and are given opportunities to build relationships by working directly with individuals, the service experience becomes more meaningful.[8]

The catalyst for moving students from seeing service as fun to a more complex perspective occurs when they realize that what they do makes a difference. Students see this when they are connected in every phase of the service experience, from planning and decision making to implementation and evaluation. When they have choice and control, they are naturally more invested.

Teachers contribute to fostering meaningful service experiences through strong curriculum connections, youth voice, and guided reflection. After studying about Haiti's political, social, and environmental problems, my students selected different ways to provide assistance each year, from donating school supplies to purchasing pigs for families and contributing to a clean water project. Through reflection we discussed the effects of these projects on the families and on Haiti's overall situation and envisioned what more they could do. While the students believed their efforts met important, real needs, they realized it would do little to solve the country's many problems.

By compartmentalizing the time frame, students saw their present efforts as meaningful and realized they could do more now by continuing to educate themselves and others and by searching out other Haitian relief projects in their churches or communities. In addition, they could foresee themselves doing more by advocating and voting for supportive candidates or by volunteering abroad. This bridging the gap between what can be done now and what will be done later helps students feel authentic by keeping their values aligned with their present actions and future intentions.

Progress Monitoring and Process Monitoring

Research shows that collecting information on student progress as well as the teaching and learning process helps identify effective strategies connected to student and program outcomes. Using the data gathered to identify and correct problems and enhance instruction improves academic skills and student motivation.[9]

Documentation and evaluation of student, program, and community outcomes, as well as assessment of process and procedures, forms the core of effective programs and leads to continuous improvement. Just as in lesson planning, monitoring service-learning programs requires having clear goals and outcomes for students, the program, and the community; an identified implementation plan to achieve the outcomes; and an assessment plan to collect quantitative data (surveys, quizzes, and tests) and qualitative data (reflection, essays, focus groups, interviews). Effective monitoring should be ongoing, varied, and repeated over time for gauging longitudinal trends and impact. Administrators and teachers need to analyze and synthesize the data, interpret the results, and make modifications to improve student and program outcomes.

The Search Institute's Profiles of Student Life: Attitudes and Behaviors is a good survey for gauging students' beliefs, attitudes, and activities in a wide range of areas that are often identified by service-learning practitioners as student and program outcomes. Examples include connection to community, engagement in service, self-efficacy, wellness, diversity, and leadership. The results are invaluable for monitoring outcomes and setting improvement goals.

Using focus groups with students, community agencies, teachers, and parents is a relatively easy method that produces meaningful feedback and fresh perspectives for validation and improvement. A very common practice is to conduct a *SWOT analysis* where the group highlights "strengths, weaknesses, opportunities, and threats" in regard to the service-learning program. Another, perhaps simpler, approach is to ask two questions: what's working well? and what's not?

A technique that improves feedback and ensures that all voices are heard is to begin the focus group with time for silent brainstorming, during which participants reflect on a question or theme and write their thoughts on note cards. After they have composed their thoughts and written their reflections, the facilitator begins the discussion. Collecting the note cards after the session provides additional feedback by gathering thoughts that were not verbalized.

Students can also take the lead in monitoring programs and process, especially when the goals are collectively set and agreed to by the group. Before students departed for a two-week service trip to Guatemala working with Nuestros Pequeños Hermanos, one goal they set was to live simply and in solidarity with the children they would be helping—so they agreed not to bring/use cell phones, iPods, and other luxury electronics. Every morning and evening the group met for student-led reflection and discussion, and one evening students voiced a concern that a few people (who remained nameless) on the trip were not adhering to this goal and invited them to reconsider and recommit to the purpose of the trip.

Duration

Research shows that when students participate in service-learning projects over longer periods of time, academic, civic, and character-development outcomes are stronger. Billig's review of research suggests that meeting these long-term goals requires at least a semester or seventy hours devoted to planning, preparing, action, and reflection.[10]

All teachers know growth, skill building, and personal development take time. To arrive at deep learning and reach attitudinal and behavioral student outcomes requires more than "covering the material" and "doing some service." Students need time to become more informed on issues, problem solve, make connections between service and course content, assess, and reflect. Similarly, developing relationships with those they are serving and seeing the impact of their service occurs over time. There are various paths to designing service experiences that have sufficient duration, such as offering service-based classes; having an academic department commit to an ongoing relationship with a community agency that aligns with its content area; and encouraging students to continue their service work after the course ends.

Service-learning is most powerful when connected to the mission of the school and integrated into the curriculum and culture of the institution. When service is seen as a core component of school life, students can develop their skills, understandings, and perspectives over the span of years (four to six years) at that institution through courses, schoolwide projects, and service through clubs, activities, and athletics. Students both reinforce and transfer knowledge and skills when they move from one service-learning experience to another project in a different course. As students become adept at the steps and processes, they can initiate their own projects and transform extracurricular teams' and clubs' community-service projects into service-learning experiences. This all-school approach lays the foundation for a lifetime commitment to community engagement.

Reciprocal Partnerships

Research shows that when community partners and the school or university see their relationship as mutually beneficial and engage in conversation and planning to meet the needs of both entities, service-learning flourishes.[11]

Community partners are vital to successful service-learning programs, and, as in all relationships, communication is key. Both sides need to explain their backgrounds, beliefs, and goals; be open about expectations and limitations; be reflective about the ongoing service experiences; and be honest in their feedback. Extending hospitality and gratitude helps foster a strong, enduring affiliation.

We often overlook the role community partners have in teaching our students. When teachers communicate the learning and developmental goals for the students, the community teacher can amplify the message and demonstrate concrete examples and applications to the students, making learning more integrated in the total experience. In addition, when students work alongside adults at agencies committed to social-justice outcomes, they see what it means to live a life in which beliefs and actions are integrated. In these role models, students envision future possibilities for themselves.

One of our most successful community partnerships is with Perspectives Family Center, a residential program working to improve the quality of life for homeless and at-risk families. Our students participate in a variety of after-school activities with the children, including Kids' Café Dinner and Kids' Connection. One day the volunteer coordinator telephoned our service coordinator about our students. She said they were great, but she did not understand why they would want to start new clubs with the children or begin art classes. Our service-learning coordinator offered to present a workshop for Perspectives' staff on service-learning. The staff starting thinking about service-learning and decided that if it was good for these high-school students, it would be really great for their children; and with the help of a minigrant from our school, they incorporated service-learning into their programs.

Standards of Quality Service-Learning

Service-learning researchers, educators, and practitioners have long worked together to identify the characteristics of effective service-learning. In 1967, Sigmon and Ramsey first coined the term *service-learning* at the Southern Regional Education Board (SREB), and then in 1969 the board collaborated to write the earliest definition of service-learning in 1969: "connecting student learning opportunities to community service and social change."[12]

A decade later, SREB elaborated on the principles of reciprocity and mutuality supporting Sigmon's three principles of service-learning: "those being served control the service(s) provided; those being served become better able to serve and be served by their own actions; [and] those who serve are also learners and have significant control over what is expected to learn."[14] In 1989, the Wingspread Conference gathered together thirty-three pioneers in service-learning, who were advocates, scholars, and practitioners, to reflect on its origins, practices, and future. At the center of all their programs was a desire to connect theory and practice, schools and community, and thought and action. Early exemplary service programs included social analysis and social justice.[15]

Shelly Billig, RMC Resource Corporation,[16] and Wokie Weah, National Youth Leadership Council (NYLC),[17] have coordinated the most recent efforts to identify principles of effective practice, which resulted in K–12

Table 6.1. K–12 Service-Learning Standards for Quality Practices

MEANINGFUL SERVICE

Service-learning actively engages participants in meaningful and personally relevant service activities.

Indicators:
1. Service-learning experiences are appropriate to participant ages and developmental abilities.
2. Service-learning addresses issues that are personally relevant to the participants.
3. Service-learning provides participants with interesting and engaging service activities.
4. Service-learning encourages participants to understand their service experiences in the context of the underlying societal issues being addressed.
5. Service-learning leads to attainable and visible outcomes that are valued by those being served.

LINK TO CURRICULUM

Service-learning is intentionally used as an instructional strategy to meet learning goals and/or content standards.

Indicators:
1. Service-learning has clearly articulated learning goals.
2. Service-learning is aligned with the academic and/or programmatic curriculum.
3. Service-learning helps participants learn now to transfer knowledge and skills from one setting to another.
4. Service-learning that takes place in schools is formally recognized in school board policies and student records.

REFLECTION

Service-learning incorporates multiple challenging reflection activities that are ongoing and that prompt deep thinking and analysis about oneself and one's relationship to society.

Indicators:
1. Service-learning reflection includes a variety of verbal, written, artistic, and nonverbal activities to demonstrate understanding and changes in participants' knowledge, skills, and/or attitudes.
2. Service-learning reflection occurs before, during, and after the service experience.
3. Service-learning reflection prompts participants to think deeply about complex community problems and alternative solutions.

(*continued*)

Table 6.1. (*continued*)

4. Service-learning reflection encourages participants to examine their preconceptions and assumptions in order to explore and understand their roles and responsibilities as citizens.
5. Service-learning reflection encourages participants to examine a variety of social and civic issues related to their service-learning experience so that participants understand connections to public policy and civic life.

DIVERSITY

Service-learning promotes understanding of diversity and mutual respect among all participants.

Indicators:
1. Service-learning helps participants identify and analyze different points of view to gain understanding of multiple perspectives.
2. Service-learning helps participants develop interpersonal skills in conflict resolution and group decision-making.
3. Service-learning helps participants actively seek to understand and value the diverse backgrounds and perspectives of those offering and receiving service.
4. Service-learning encourages participants to recognize and overcome stereotypes.

YOUTH VOICE

Service-learning provides youth with a strong voice in planning, implementing, and evaluating service-learning experiences with guidance from adults.

Indicators:
1. Service-learning engages youth in generating ideas during the planning, implementation, and evaluation processes.
2. Service-learning involves youth in the decision-making process throughout the service-learning experiences.
3. Service-learning involves youth and adults in creating an environment that supports trust and open expression of ideas.
4. Service-learning promotes acquisition of knowledge and skills to enhance youth leadership and decision-making.
5. Service-learning involves youth in evaluating the quality and effectiveness of the service-learning experience.

PARTNERSHIPS

Service-learning partnerships are collaborative, mutually beneficial, and address community needs.

Indicators:
1. Service-learning involves a variety of partners, including youth, educators, families, community members, community-based organizations, and/or businesses.

2. Service-learning partnerships are characterized by frequent and regular communication to keep all partners well-informed about activities and progress.
3. Service-learning partners collaborate to establish a shared vision and set common goals to address community needs.
4. Service-learning partners collaboratively develop and implement action plans to meet specified goals.
5. Service-learning partners share knowledge and understanding of school and community assets and needs, and view each other as valued resources.

PROGRESS MONITORING

Service-learning engages participants in an ongoing process to assess the quality of implementation and progress toward meeting specified goals, and uses results for improvement and sustainability.

Indicators:
1. Service-learning participants collect evidence of progress toward meeting specific service goals and learning outcomes from multiple sources throughout the service- learning experience.
2. Service-learning participants collect evidence of the quality of service-learning implementation from multiple sources throughout the service-learning experience.
3. Service-learning participants use evidence to improve service-learning experiences.
4. Service-learning participants communicate evidence of progress toward goals and outcomes with the broader community, including policy-makers and education leaders, to deepen service-learning understanding and ensure that high quality practices are sustained.

DURATION AND INTENSITY

Service-learning has sufficient duration and intensity to address community needs and meet specified outcomes.

Indicators:
1. Service-learning experiences include the processes of investigating community needs, preparing for service, action, reflection, demonstration of learning and impacts, and celebration.
2. Service-learning is conducted during concentrated blocks of time across a period of several weeks or months.
3. Service-learning experiences provide enough time to address identified community needs and achieve learning outcomes.

Source: K–12 Service-Learning Standards for Quality Practice, © 2008 by the National Youth Leadership Council, at www.nylc.org. Reprinted with permission.

Service-Learning Standards for Quality Practices in 2008. Crafting the standards involved broad participation over several years and grew out of a synthesis of research and professional judgments. The framework presents eight standards and thirty-five indicators or predictors of high-impact programs that have implications for practitioners, researchers, and policy makers.[18]

Research shows that through curriculum integration, ongoing cognitively challenging reflection activities, incorporation of youth voice, respect for diversity, meaningful service projects, progress monitoring and process monitoring, appropriate program duration, and reciprocal partnerships in the community, secondary schools can implement service-learning programs with positive student outcomes. In chapter 7, we will delve a little deeper into merging critical-consciousness development with service learning.

CHAPTER SEVEN

Higher Education: Strategies for Critical-Consciousness Development

It is not our role to speak to the people about our own view of the world, not to attempt to impose that view on them, but rather to dialogue with the people about their view and ours.

—Paulo Freire[1]

Throughout the last thirty years, I have had many recurring educational questions, but one in particular has continued to provoke me: How can I "move" people in their thinking? As I became more critically aware, I wanted everyone to know what I knew and see the inherent injustices in our economic, social, and political systems. I wanted to help others see how entrenched policies and practices maintain the status quo, providing advantages to dominant groups and disadvantages to groups suffering discrimination based on race, class, gender, age, religion, sexual orientation, and ability.

After reading Paulo Freire's work, I realized that students need to go through the same discovery process as I did: you can't just give them the answer. As educators, we cannot unveil the world for others. What we can do is help initiate the process of unveiling by posing problems, sparking discussion, and providing factual information. My question evolved: How can teachers help students develop a critical awareness of their world, build empathy, and create a desire to change society?

In this chapter, I describe the teaching methods and student outcomes of a graduate course entitled Infusing Multiculturalism and Critical Pedagogy in Catholic Schools. I begin by walking through strategies used to foster student critical-consciousness development and describing how scaffolding the course content contributed to strong student outcomes. This course was offered to a group of twenty Catholic elementary and secondary teachers enrolled in the master of arts program in curriculum and instruction at the University of St. Thomas's Murray Institute. For the course design, I drew upon the work of many authors and educators, various teaching strategies, and my own educational experiences, to create a course that would empower educators with knowledge and a motivation to implement an educational praxis for social justice. In addition, I applied the theoretical framework for critical-consciousness development described in chapters 4–5.

This course extended throughout the school year, meeting one Saturday per month for six hours. These class periods allowed me to design lessons that delved deeper into topics and to include activities such as role-playing, which are often difficult to accommodate in traditional class periods. The stranded class schedule brought other significant benefits: the extended time between class meetings resulted in students having more time to devote to the assignments, reflect deeper on the various topics, and try out new prac-tices in their own classes. Students need adequate time to process new in-formation and ideas when they are learning new topics such as multicultural education and critical pedagogy. Because we are not simply asking students to learn the content surrounding issues of race, class, gender, oppression, and privilege, but are inviting them to a personal conversion through which they see the world differently, individual inquiry and the resulting emotional ele-ments require nurturing.

This course was designed to challenge participants to reflect on teaching and education as social justice in action. The objectives were to seek a deeper understanding of multiculturalism and critical pedagogy and their implica-tions for the classroom; to understand the historical and social construction of race and Whiteness and how their effects are manifested in schools and society today; and to see ourselves, others, social issues, and our potential to make change.

Course methods and activities modeled elements of critical pedagogy: stu-dents cocreated the curriculum and their own knowledge through dialogue with others and reflections on texts and experiences; the teacher functioned as a problem poser; the subject matter was meaningful; and time was pro-vided for critical thought and reflection. These practices align well with several research-based practices of effective service-learning programs pre-sented in chapter 8, including curriculum integration, reflection, and student voice. These strategies also facilitate the progression of critical-consciousness development described in chapters 4–5, which show how students navigate the stages. While the service component in this course was a one-time occurrence, the preservice preparation, service, and reflection connected class material to real world experiences, which, in conjunction with course material, resulted in increased student understanding of self, others, social issues, and their potential to make a difference.

Incorporating Critical-Pedagogy Practices

Critical pedagogy, as first outlined by Freire in *Pedagogy of the Oppressed*, seeks to empower students and teachers with the critical thinking skills necessary to bring about social change by developing a critical consciousness and a will to act in solidarity with the oppressed.[2] This pedagogy provides a framework for educators to create a more democratic classroom, where students are the Subjects who are engaged in meaningful subject matter and construct their knowledge through active investigation, critical reflection, and action. The content is student-generated and connects to their lives and their communities. In traditional settings, many educational experiences have relied primarily on what Freire terms "banking education," in which teachers are the Subjects, and students become the Objects of education: the empty receptacles to be filled with the gift of knowledge. In this course I attempted to incorporate best practices for an empowering education in which the students and I were both Subjects in learning.

In *Empowering Education*, Ira Shor describes methods for implementing a critical pedagogy practice in American schools. With a goal of promoting critical awareness in students, I drew upon four of Shor's educational strategies: situated learning, dialogic discourse, teachers as problem posers, and activist learning. Situated learning is based in the lives and interests of students, who become cocreators of the curriculum by raising issues that concern them. The curriculum evolves through student and teacher negotiation rather than a traditional textbook- and teacher-driven curriculum. Dialogic discourse is a democratic, participatory process, which results in the construction of knowledge, and teachers as "problem-posers" take on the role of facilitators to student discovery.[3] By generating questions, you will guide the students as they critically analyze the world. Finally, activist learning challenges students to investigate the present and the past, create a vision of a more just world, and actively work to create it. Students must connect their critical reflection to social action in order to become change agents.[4] As an outcome of reflection, dialogic discourse, and problem posing, students' consciousness is raised, and they become more critical in their analyses. This opens the path to transformative action.

From the outset, I wanted to model critical pedagogy in my instructional methods and class activities and encourage students to reflect continuously on what they were learning as well as the methods we were using. I also wanted to stress the importance of critical reflection, analysis, and dialogue in the critical-pedagogy learning process. To accomplish this goal there was a series of recurring questions that we addressed at each session:

- How does this apply to me personally?
- How does this apply to me as a teacher and to my students?
- How does this apply to me as a member of the educational community?
- How does this apply to me as a member of a global society?

The recurring questions not only helped connect what they were learning in the classroom to their lives, their worldviews, and their educational practice, but also served to make the learning connections more explicit by including them in written and/or verbal reflection.

Cocreating the Curriculum: Situated Learning

Beginning with a general framework of the course content and process, I wanted to engage students in further developing the course and make the material relevant to their personal and professional lives. The Freirean concept that all learning should be generated from the students' lives and concerns worked well for his adult literacy work in Brazil, but often does not translate easily to the American educational system. Building on Freire's belief that each culture must develop practices according to its needs, Ira Shor expanded the model to include not only student themes (*generative*), but also teacher themes (*topical*) to raise important issues that would not necessarily occur to students, and scholastic themes (*academic*) relating to specific content-related knowledge.[5] Overall, I tried to create a balance of curriculum development by thirds: one-third teacher created, one-third student created, and one third cocreated. Cocreating the curriculum honored students' voices and leadership in constructing a meaningful, relevant course tailored to their needs. Strategies used included student inventory cards, critical-incident questionnaires (CIQs), and individual student-led activities.

Student Inventory Cards

The first day of class I asked students to write down topics they wanted to address in the course and their questions regarding the topics on the syllabus. These topics and questions (table 7.1) were woven into the curriculum in discussions, activities, and assignments.

Table 7.1. Class Questions, Student Inventory Cards, and Online Postings

Content

How do we incorporate multicultural education (MC), Catholic social teachings (CST) and social justice in the classroom?

What are realistic expectations? Do we have to teach them directly?

How do we make ties to CST/MC when they are not readily apparent, e.g., math, science?

What is the difference between CST and social justice?

How do you incorporate service-learning in the classroom?

Process

How do you create a democratic classroom for younger kids?

How do you increase awareness of justice and injustice with younger kids?

How do we move from charity to justice? Benevolent, but not generous.

How can we empower kids?

How do we inspire creativity and develop critical thinkers?

Environment

How can we discuss diversity issues without offending?

How do you create respect for diversity in a homogeneous environment?

How should you deal with a racist third-grader? With students' resistance, e.g., laughing about poverty?

How can we help ESL students and their families?

Larger Scope

How do you make changes in your department/school? How to convince others to do it?

Understanding affirmative action

Understanding multicultural education

Contradictions in the church regarding role of women, sexual orientation and CST

Critical-Incident Questionnaires

At the end of every class, students were asked to give feedback on the class using a questionnaire (table 7.2) adapted from Stephen Brookfield's questionnaire in *On Becoming a Reflective Practitioner*.[6] Weaving this throughout the course served several purposes. First, I received feedback on students' expectations and suggestions on content, structure, and process. Second, the CIQs provided a bridge between monthly class meetings, allowing us to address lingering questions from the previous month and segue into new topics. I also used their comments to assess how they viewed themselves and their roles as educators, thereby detecting any frustrations or challenges requiring analysis.

Table 7.2. Critical Incident Questionnaire

Please take a few minutes to respond to each of the questions below about today's class. Don't put your name on the form—your responses are anonymous. When you have finished writing, put it on the table by the door. At the start of next class, I will be sharing the responses with the group. Thanks for taking the time to do this. What you write will help me make the class more responsive to your concerns.

1. At what moment in the class did you feel the most engaged with what was happening?
2. At what moment in the class did you feel the most distanced from what was happening?
3. What new learning emerged for you from readings, class discussions, or activities?
4. What questions or challenges do you still have? What new questions emerged?
5. How will your new knowledge, insights, or understandings impact your teaching? Did you make a commitment to change some aspect of what you do?

Cocreating the Learning Experience

In addition to attending all class sessions and participating critically in class discussion and group work, students were required to select one of several options to cocreate the learning experience. They could begin the class by leading a multicultural reflection or prayer, or find a related current event or controversy to use as a "hot topic" discussion during lunch. Topics included the following:

- the question of whether pharmacists should have the right to refuse to dispense prescriptions that conflict with their religious beliefs or values, such as contraception or the "morning-after pill"
- the growing practice of White college students throwing "ghetto" or "gangsta" parties dressed to mimic stereotypes of Black people
- Florida's new law (2006) declaring that American history shall be viewed as factual and must be taught as prescribed, and may not be interpreted or questioned
- Father Jon Nilson's article "Racist Like Me"

Constructing Knowledge: Dialogic Discourse

Constructing knowledge requires placing students at the center of the curriculum and encouraging them to make sense of the world. Critical pedagogy recognizes that students are not empty vessels needing to be filled, but rather arrive with a wealth of knowledge accumulated through their lived experiences. Unlike the banking view of education, which minimizes and inhibits students' creative power, this strategy develops critical thinking, fosters their ability to question the status quo, and encourages them to build a critical view of the world. I wanted to tap into the students' collective knowledge and then stretch it with additional information, reflection, questions, and discussion, provoking new knowledge and deeper understandings of their own values, beliefs, attitudes, and behaviors, as well as the world around them. Methods included using student collaborative thoughts and writings as a textbook, and utilizing Brookfield's Good Practice Audit.

Student Writing as Textbook

Because we spent a considerable amount of time discussing readings and viewpoints in small and large groups, it was important to pull the various strands together to formalize the students' thoughts and articulate what they had learned. Between classes, students posted their reflections online on our class discussion board, which I often used to create a document synthesizing their collective thoughts and the knowledge constructed. This is a good alternative to having all the small groups report back to the whole group after a discussion. Table 7.3 is a composite of all the postings after a class session on multicultural education, responding to the following questions: What is multicultural education? What are some excuses for why we don't do it and some inaccurate myths people have about multicultural education?

Good Practice Audit

A thread that was carried throughout the class began on the first day with Brookfield's Good Practice Audit.[7] This exercise taps into students' past educational experiences to reflect on and isolate examples of positive and negative learning situations. This encourages students to consider what they believe about good education and what they want to incorporate into their practices.

In this activity, students completed a matrix of the worst and best educational experiences that they'd had in their own lives; that they had observed or heard about in the experiences of friends or colleagues; and that they had experienced as teachers. They then reflected on what made each experience bad or good. After all six scenarios were written, students met in small groups to share their memories and identify characteristics that they believed led to good education. The group lists were collected, compiled, and redistributed to the class at the next meeting. As we continued to build new awareness

Table 7.3. Student Writing as Textbook: The Sum Is Greater Than the Parts

SUMMARY OF ONLINE POSTINGS

Definitions: Multicultural education (is) . . .

seeing reality from multiple perspectives, not just from the dominant
  perspectives

antiracist education

addresses power relations

about understanding oneself and others in community

learning about one's own culture

examines history/concepts/current events from multiple perspectives

involves consistent and honest dialogue that aims toward a better
  understanding of others

examines why some people are more fortunate than others

examines why there are prejudices and stereotypes and how and why they are
  formed

understanding the various differences (racial, ethnic, religious, etc.) among
  people in our home, school, community and world

about breaking down stereotypes

an attempt to end the oppression of those who are not in the dominant class

learning about other cultures and other people in order to understand and
  respect our similarities and differences

a philosophy and a process

Beliefs and attitudes: Multicultural education (is) . . .

our responsibility

requires teachers to review curriculum and research different ways of teaching

can take place anywhere

sounds good to everyone, but is rarely truly embraced because of its
  complexity

best interwoven into all aspects of schools

important to understand even if (especially if) you have limited (no) contact
  with "others"

needs teachers to collaborate more with colleagues to develop curriculum

an ongoing process . . . there is always room to grow

needs to address all forms of oppression, e.g., gender issues, racism, classism,
  ageism, etc.

a monumental job in homogeneous rural communities

difficult because communities are segregated, which creates fear of "others"

needs to go beyond token activities such as multicultural weeks and
  assemblies on ethnic dances

Excuses and rationalizing: People don't "do" multicultural education because . . .

it is hard to do and takes time

teachers lack knowledge and experiences to implement it effectively

it's not necessary in a homogenous community

teachers don't have time and resources

there will always be prejudice and discrimination
it won't solve society's problems
it's hard to change attitudes

Negative (or inaccurate) views: Multicultural education (is) . . .
just one more "thing" put on teachers
can bring resistance from parents and community
often represents other groups only in the role of victims
about bilingual education which inhibits learning English
about cultural "tourism"
easier now because textbooks include diversity
"waters down" the curriculum

Student quotes
"For at its best multiculturalism addresses power relations, asks the difficult
   questions, requires self-reflection and most importantly the call to action to
   end suffering."
"Schools don't do enough to stop kids from making racist comments."
"Perfection is not a place to exist but a direction to yearn for."
"Multicultural education is more about seeking alternative viewpoints than
   learning about specific cultures."
"People are afraid of the unknown."
"Members of dominant groups come up with many 'rational sounding'
   reasons not to support it."
"Since we live in such a diverse world, students need to learn how to work,
   cooperate, and appreciate those who are different than them and not to
   judge others because of their differences."
"Multicultural education is an educational process that stresses the
   development of critical thinking skills, understanding of others points
   of view, preparation for knowledgeable participation in the democratic
   process, and action to work for social justice. The reason we need
   multicultural education is to prepare students for a changing nation in
   which more and more of the population will be from diverse, non-White
   cultures and for a changing world in which the realities of technology and
   economy tie us closer daily to far-flung corners of the world."

and knowledge in the subsequent classes on Catholic social teachings; multicultural education; critical pedagogy; race, racism, and White privilege; and service-learning, the chart of characteristics continued to develop. A careful reading of the final composite (table 7.4) reveals the impact of the various topics discussed through the course of the year.

Teacher's Role: Teachers as Problem Posers
In a critical-pedagogy classroom, the teacher plays the vital role of designing the activity/experience, facilitating the postreflection discussion,

Table 7.4. What Characterizes Good Education?

FINAL COMPOSITE OF YEAR-LONG INSIGHT

Content

application, connection to real life

addresses reality with controversy/conflict

connects to students' experiences

integrates multiculturalism across the curriculum

opens windows to other experiences

in-depth examination of cultures & perspectives

addresses social-economic classes

expands curriculum to include more perspectives

presents multiple perspectives, especially those often omitted or misrepresented

corrects misconceptions & miseducation

examines beliefs, myths, principles, & practices & how they influence society

examines the dominant culture & how it gets buy-in to its values & practices; White privilege, power relations

teacher's & students' Whiteness as a culture

history of race & racism, & current manifestations

presents Black & White antiracists as role models

Process/Teaching Style

flexible groups, day-to-day grouping

cooperative & collaborative

variation of instruction, hands-on activities

discussion

good pace of class & activities

students have choice

fosters questioning; questions status quo

enables people to understand & operate within cultures different from their own

uses role-playing to lead to discussion

reflections, journals

students research issues

critical thinking

students are active & engaged

critical analysis of ideology, practices, real conditions of students' lives & societal norms

facilitates students' discovery of the effects of oppression in the United States & the world

uses students' experiences as a source of learning

gives students opportunities to "practice" using their voices

asks who benefits? is it fair?

compares & contrasts new information to prior knowledge.

shares power with students

incorporates service-learning

Environment/Relationship

fosters personal relationship with & among students

care & respect

high expectations

inclusive, embrace diverse personalities & perspectives

gives positive feedback

good communication

teachers/students as collaborative team

empowering students

be open to conflict & controversy

multicultural environment (bulletin boards, etc.)

the whole school/parents understand & embrace multiculturalism

treats all with dignity

challenges prejudices

antiprofiling (antiracist, antisexist, etc.)

builds courage to stand up for what is right, to take action for justice

fosters students' positive feelings about themselves & their heritage.

empowers students through service-learning

inclusive, students see themselves in curriculum

Teacher Characteristics

reflects deeply on decisions made; selecting curriculum: why we teach what

is always evolving in understanding, knowledge, & classroom instruction/methods

models how to combat hegemony

is open to change—particularly student-driven

is always aware of his/her power in the classroom & how he/she uses it

loves content, passionate, but also sees the students as more important than content

flexible, organized

approachable, open to student concerns, accepts feedback

spends time in collaboration with colleagues for planning & professional discussions

realizes his/her class isn't the only thing students are dealing with

knows kids & family

teacher as facilitator

educates self about own culture & others'

collaborates with & is open with parents

teaches by example, volunteering

tries to develop critical consciousness in self & students

validates claim of racism; assumes it is always about race; is not on the defensive

acknowledges White privilege

addresses racist, sexist language, jokes, etc.

and creating a safe environment in which all voices are heard. Problem posing is a powerful and engaging teaching strategy that develops critical thought. As students address real-life concerns, they begin to see the world critically. Inquiry, reflection, research, and analysis are all components that lead students not only to see the world how it is now and how it was in the past, but also to envision how it could be in the future. As Freire explains, "In the problem-posing education, people develop their power to perceive critically the way they exist in the world with which and in which they find themselves: they come to see the world not as a static reality, but as a reality in process and in transformation."[8]

As teachers remove themselves from center stage, they create space for students to grapple with big ideas as they construct their own new knowledge and articulate their worldview, which promotes developing a critical consciousness. As our teaching role becomes more like that of an educational guide encouraging and directing students, our work and responsibility remain significant. Teaching strategies to increase student learning include selecting and posing questions that provoke thought and, when necessary, redirect discussions; and back-loading to fill in missing information or correct errors. Using a third medium, such as films or role-playing, is an effective teaching tool both as a source of information and as a context for reflection.

Selecting and Posing Questions

Provocative questions were built into the course design and became the point of departure for creating new knowledge, as seen in the recurring syllabus questions, the framing question for each class session, and student inventory cards. Typically, I would open a topic by tapping into what the students already knew or felt about an issue, and, as they expanded their knowledge base through readings and discussions, more questions would emerge.

The student comments and questions from the CIQs and the Blackboard online discussion boards were sources for additional problem posing, which we addressed at the beginning of the subsequent class period. I looked for general themes or areas of misunderstanding, checked for any bias or inaccurate assumptions in student responses, and then formulated additional questions to raise the level of critical thinking.

For example, after gaining a better understanding of multicultural education through a study of its different stages of implementation, new questions emerged, regarding such issues as their school's position in multicultural-education implementation; who had the power; how decisions were made, and what individuals could do to influence/inform colleagues.

Back-Loading Information

Shor's model includes an avenue for teachers to share their knowledge and expertise in a way that enhances student thinking rather than diminishes it. The learning process begins with initial questions and reflections, in which students respond in written format or small-group discussions. Students then interact with documents, readings, films, and other media and add to their previous knowledge. Teachers readdress student questions to the group at large or pose an additional question that leads to new insights. If students are struggling with concepts, teachers offer their own insights by back-loading information, theory, or opinions. *Back-loading* is different from *front-loading*, such as with lectures, because students have had the opportunity to think critically and creatively and formulate their own thoughts. Back-loading serves to help students refine and build on their understanding.

For example, students were confused about the concept of "banking" education. They understood and agreed with Freire's belief that it was counter to the aim of education, but they were struggling with whether lecturing was always bad. They wondered if all teachers who bank knowledge are oppressive. I asked them to reflect on the characteristics of banking education and what creates an oppressive practice. They concluded that giving lectures, setting rules, or having behavioral expectations are not wrong and are often appropriate and necessary.

It was then that I entered my thoughts into the discussion, saying that it is more about the attitude that you bring into the classroom than about giving a lecture. How do you treat students? Do you value their experience as knowledge? Do you raise them up and challenge them to think? I also shared insights I had learned from Gloria Ladson-Billings as she discussed the role of White teachers in diverse classrooms, answering her students' questions on how you do multicultural education. She pointed out that "'doing' is less important than 'being' . . . practicing culturally relevant pedagogy is one of the ways of 'being' that will inform ways of 'doing.'"[9]

Using a Third Medium

The empowering feature of problem posing is that students create their own knowledge based on their experiences, information, reflection, and discussion. It removes teachers from the center and limits the potential of creating situations where teachers promote their own political views without giving students the opportunity to grapple with the issue themselves. Another strategy I use to ensure that students are at the center of their learning process is to incorporate a third medium.

In the traditional classroom, interaction is generally between the student and teacher. Using a third medium, such as role-playing, interviews, film, narratives, readings, community members, or service-learning, allows students to engage actively in experiences that have the potential to change their awareness, build empathy, and create a desire to advocate for change. By using a third medium, our teaching role becomes one of creating a catalyst for students to gain information and reflect. Students are empowered to think critically, create their own view of how the world should be, and begin to work to build it. Modeling the use of a third medium in this course included guest speakers, the Intercultural Developmental Inventory assessment, the film *Race: The Power of an Illusion*, and a service-learning experience.

One of the most engaging and effective activities we did as a class was a role-play on the purpose of education and the power dynamics between the various stakeholders. Using Bill Bigelow's role-play Testing, Tracking, and Toeing the Line,[10] students learned about the origins of the modern high school and how school reforms set into motion educational practices that ensured social reproduction and maintained the status quo. As students actively engaged in their roles, they constructed knowledge and discovered what is felt like to be an immigrant, a Black activist, or a union worker, as opposed to a corporate executive or a White, middle-class parent. The debriefing discussion showed me how this learning was much more powerful and longer lasting than traditional instruction.

Service-Learning: Activist Learning

Shor describes how critical pedagogy is activism by its very nature "in critical questioning of the status quo, in its participatory methods, and in its insistence that knowledge is not fixed, but constantly changing."[11] Freire further explains how problem posing and reflection lead to action. As students continue to discuss problems relevant to them and their world, they feel the need to respond to the current situation and end the suffering.[12] Interrogating the status quo, shining light on the realities of injustice, and critically reflecting are all acts that transform self and society. Service-learning is a vehicle for teachers and students to take activism to the next level by engaging in the community for social change.

Service-learning is a strategy in which students have leadership roles in thoughtfully organized service experiences that meet real needs in the community. The service is integrated into the students' academic studies with structured time to research, reflect, discuss, and connect experiences to learning and their worldviews. Service-learning, like critical pedagogy, is based in learning about community need, critically reflecting, and taking action. The level and type of community engagement is a reflection of where individuals are currently located in their critical-consciousness development. In this course, students researched poverty and homelessness and then prepared and served meals at an adult drop-in center, after which there was group discussion and individual reflection. Due to the time spent learning and reflecting, the service-learning experience had a powerful impact on the students, which advanced them in their critical-consciousness development.

Critical Consciousness Development and Student Outcomes

Using the road map to critical-consciousness development outlined in chapters 4 and 5 as the theoretical framework, coupled with critical-pedagogy practices, I was deliberate in the design and delivery of the course with the end goal of supporting students as they became more critically aware. The progression of topics, course activities, and assignments was intentionally planned to create a democratic classroom in which students would foster a greater awareness of themselves, others, and society while developing a greater commitment to social justice.

I sought to incorporate stage-appropriate information, experiences, and reflection opportunities to promote growth and support students as they moved through stages of critical-consciousness development. A general curricular scaffold begins with time to reflect on core values and personal beliefs; then, through a variety of input, students become informed and begin to develop a more accurate view of reality; they then experience cognitive dissonance due to contradictions; and finally they imagine possibilities and commit to creating change.

The course began with students identifying and articulating their beliefs and responsibilities to others. Then we investigated the contradictions between what we, as individuals and as a society, say we believe in and what is actually occurring. Fostering a desire to align actions and beliefs is the catalyst for moving into the final stage of critical-consciousness development, which emanates from caring deeply about justice and making a personal commitment to work for change.

Although the students began and finished the course at different developmental points, throughout the course they all showed a commitment to critical reflection and grew in their ability to view the world critically. As their reflections demonstrated, they developed a deeper awareness of themselves, others, and social issues, and became more committed to action for justice. The next sections describe strategies used to address areas of concentration in this course.

Catholic Social Teachings: Can Schools Be Countercultural?

The course began with articles and activities that provoked students to think about what they believed and their responsibilities to act on their beliefs. What are the characteristics of a great school? A great teacher? What are they called to be and do in the classroom and in the world? Because the Murray Institute has a specifically Catholic mission, we used Catholic social

Text Box 7.1

CIQ Student Comments: Impact on Teaching and Personal Commitments

- "Whew . . . I am overwhelmed and appreciative of everything. I have a better understanding of how to implement what I feel God's been calling me to do with my whole life and why."
- "Do I have the skills to effectively embrace Catholic social teaching and critical pedagogy in my classroom and my school? Where am I headed?"
- "I was challenged in discussing Catholic as being 'welcoming' and 'community-based.' How welcoming are we? Who do we not welcome?"
- "How is it okay for the Church to teach social justice, yet be so sexist?"
- "I made a commitment to change my attitude in my classroom."
- "I truly don't do a lot of work with CST currently, but after today's discussion I will attempt to incorporate these regularly."

teachings and readings from theologian Thomas Groome's *Educating for Life* as foundational works from which to build their new knowledge and classroom applications.[13] For secular settings, the basic tenets of humanism, the United Nations Declaration of Universal Human Rights, and the U.S. Declaration of Independence, Constitution, and Bill of Rights serve as points of departure to discuss beliefs and responsibilities.

Multicultural Education: What Is It and Why Is It Important in Schools?

My plan for the topic of multiculturalism was to help students see the congruence between the goals of critical multiculturalism and the beliefs and goals they had collectively compiled in the previous lesson. I also wanted to demonstrate how a term could have different meanings to different people. First we read various definitions of multicultural education and discussed the theoretical frameworks of James Banks, Christine Sleeter, and Sonia Nieto. After reading articles that outlined distinct stages of multicultural education, students came to a greater understanding of multiculturalism and discussed common myths and critiques about multicultural education.[14] They grappled with defining *multiculturalism* in their own words and articulating why it is important for Catholic schools. The students also analyzed their position and their schools' position in terms of commitment, stages of implementation, school priorities, issues of power, and next steps. One of the assignments was

Text Box 7.2

CIQ Student Comments: Impact on Teaching and Personal Commitments

- "When I realized that the thing holding me back of doing more in multicultural education (doesn't fit with my curriculum and I can't add any more) is a cop out—there really is a choice I need to make and follow."
- "It affirms what I have started doing and encourages me to go further and to keep multiculturalism and its issues in my mind while I prepare lessons and teach."
- "Doing more to intersect issues in social justice with action. Giving kids opportunity to act on their values."
- "I feel the need to educate myself more on the truths of history so that I am not telling lies to my students."
- "Begin adding small pieces, which is better than not including multiculturalism in the classroom, and continue to build it into the curriculum."
- "Work for better understanding of my culture as well as my students'."

to explain to two people (one teacher and a person not in education) what multicultural education is and why it is important.

Critical Pedagogy: What Is It and What Does It Add to Our Understanding of Education?

The topic of critical pedagogy began the discussion on power, privilege, and oppression and built a foundation for subsequent sessions on racism and White privilege. Students read and discussed Freire's *Pedagogy of the Oppressed* and were presented with a brief overview of Freire, Marx, Gramsci, the Frankfurt school,[15] *critical social theory*, democratic education, and liberation theology.[16] Students worked to develop their own definition of critical

Text Box 7.3

CIQ Student Comments: Impact on Teaching and Personal Commitments

- "As a teacher it is my job to aid my student in developing skills to see reality from multiple perspectives and not just the perspective of the dominant groups."
- "Empathy for those who regularly live in oppression. I felt frustrated and a lack of hope as a Black activist. The role-play activity proved the point."
- "I am even more profoundly aware of my values and thoughts after discussing with others. I am unable to have discussions with people in my daily life because they are unaware of what I am doing."
- "The reading caused a lot of discussion at my house. The reading caused me to reflect on my own behavior and attitude."
- "Critical pedagogy calls us to deep reflection on the decisions we make. What curriculum is being taught and how and what methods are used when teaching?"
- "I have been growing in my understanding of what critical pedagogy means. I think educators are one of the key influences in guiding students to develop critical thinking skills. I hope to give my students a critical eye for what is not always easily seen and to have courage to take action when they see injustice."
- "For me critical pedagogy is a way of being—an approach to every aspect of one's life. It is multicultural, Catholic social teaching, democratic in its truest sense, examination of power anti-profiling (antiracist, antisexist) and critical thinking. It has become an ideal way of approaching my classroom. Although I often fall short, I know that I am a different teacher than I was two and a half years ago."

pedagogy and reflected on what it adds to our discussion of multicultural education and Catholic social teachings. Discussion on the text began in small groups, in which students highlighted passages they found particularly enlightening or perplexing, which were then brought back to the large group. Considerable time was devoted to the roles of teacher and student and pedagogical practices currently used in education, and to possibilities for change.

Race, Racism, and White Privilege: What Does It Have to Do with Me?
The next two class sessions were devoted to understanding the social construction of race, racism, and White privilege. I felt these sessions were the crux of understanding the social, political, and economic problems on a national and global scale. Working to expand our knowledge of oppression, power, and privilege, we began to tackle difficult questions such as the following:

- What is race? Where did the idea originate? What defines Whiteness?
- If race does not exist as a biological factor, why do we need to continue to talk about it?
- What has been your experience surrounding race?
- Does race affect your life? Why or why not? If so, in what ways?
- Why are neighborhoods, schools and workplaces still segregated forty years after the Civil Rights Act?
- Why are all the Black kids sitting together in the cafeteria?
- What am I doing as a person with power and privilege? Why don't White people do more to end racism?
- Are all White people racists? Can people of color be racists?
- What about affirmative action and reverse discrimination?
- How does internalized racism affect people of color and Whites? How do you unlearn it?

For background information on racial-identity formation, students read Beverly Tatum's *Why Are All the Black Kids Sitting Together in the Cafeteria?* To gain a deeper understanding of racism, Whiteness, and privilege, all students read Peggy McIntosh's *White Privilege: Unpacking the Invisible Knapsack* and additional chapters from Paul Kivel's *Uprooting Racism*, and Paula Rothenberg's *White Privilege*. These chapters were divided among the students to read, and later they presented their articles to each other in a jigsaw group activity. The film *Race: The Power of an Illusion* was a powerful tool that made a strong impact on students' understanding and ability to see concrete examples of how institutional racism continues to bestow benefits on

Text Box 7.4

CIQ Student Comments: Impact on Teaching and Personal Commitments

- "I feel I am better at understanding the difficulties facing students of color and I feel I can be an advocate in our school to help continue discussion about race and justice."
- "More awareness of how saying nothing about racist remarks allows it to grow. More commitment to bring up issues of race and let my students talk about race."
- "The school system is not designed to benefit all students equally. We must teach to the 'real conditions of students' lives and social norm' in order to make a true impact."
- "The realization that came when I was trying to think of a person of color to interview, that I do not really know anyone of color."
- "I need to change my closed, isolated lifestyle. I am committed to broaden my encounters with people of other cultures and races and to force myself to talk about race and listen to others."
- "My challenge is how to act on the knowledge of deliberate, institutional policies that disadvantage people of color."
- "Incorporate activism into my life personally."
- "What are people willing to give up to dismantle White privilege? People discuss big issues, but what would they give up? What would I be willing to give up? This is the real grit!"

Whites while disadvantaging people of color. We were now ready to analyze issues such as poverty, unemployment, poor educational opportunities, and immigration with a different lens.

Service-Learning: What Are the Needs of Our Community? What Can I Do?

It was time to make the connections between the classroom and the community. The next class was a service-learning experience at Catholic Charities' Branch III, a drop-in center that serves breakfast and lunch to 200–250 homeless adults in Minneapolis. Part of the class purchased ingredients, prepared breakfast for two shifts, and cleaned the kitchen, and a smaller group served lunched and cleaned after the meal. A one-time service opportunity can often be problematic and result in unintended consequences, such as reinforcing stereotypes or using the population served for one's own personal growth; however, with a solid foundation in critical multiculturalism and

Text Box 7.5

CIQ Student Comments: Impact on Teaching and Personal Commitments

Before Service Experience
- "I was extremely overwhelmed with the information I found on poverty in Minnesota. I have never really seen a homeless person where I live. My only exposure in my lifetime is seeing a few people on the side of the road with a sign asking for help."
- "I learned that families are considered to be in poverty if their incomes are below the federal poverty level of $20,000 per year for a family of four in 2006. However according to research, on average, to meet their basic needs, families need an income of twice the federal poverty level."
- "I found it interesting the many references to health care issues and how they are connected with poverty and homelessness."
- "There must be a way to more evenly distribute goods and services throughout the world."
- "Poverty is not just a lack of money, but a difficulty in finding resources, trouble providing for family needs and it also affects the education of kids deeply. It is a major issue and deserves the attention of all out of sheer respect for the dignity of all humanity."

After Service Experience
- "There were so many different types of people. Like me, my students have not experienced homelessness directly and have predetermined beliefs about what a homeless person looks and acts like."
- "I found myself putting on the shoes of the people we served. My husband has lost his job. When we discussed that we are all just a few steps away from this life I became somewhat panicked inside. It does make one realize how quickly some things change and life, as we knew it is no longer."
- "It was very eye opening for me to hear that many of the people we served had jobs, but did not make enough to cover their basic needs. I need to be more generous."
- "I felt powerlessness. The problems of homelessness and poverty are so wide spread and far reaching that solutions seem impossible. While it is easy for our students to plead ignorance to the problems of poverty, it is so clearly my job to teach them to see it and to believe it to be their job to help solve issues of poverty. Maybe this is where I can actually fight poverty and make a difference in the solution."

- "I felt saddened, humbled, fulfilled, empathetic and fortunate for the things I have. I did not anticipate the uncomfortable feeling I got at the idea of simply sitting and having a conversation with the clients present."
- "Although the charity aspect of social ministry is essential, the most important aspect of combating poverty is the justice component-legislative advocacy. As a result, my goal is to become more politically active, focusing on the issue of poverty."
- "Seeing the face of poverty a few feet away walking through the food line is a powerful thing. Every single one of the 200–250 individuals whom we served had their own story to tell. I grew curious and imagined for some it was a poor decision (or two), but for others, this outcome was not completely in their power."

knowledge about the group being served and their circumstances, the experience can show the human side of suffering and put a face on poverty.

Effective preparation was my prerequisite. To learn about poverty and homelessness in Minnesota and the United States, students' preclass assignment was to research the topic online and post their findings and sources on our online discussion board. Many students were shocked by the statistics and humbled by our collective ignorance on the topic. We also viewed a documentary, *Land of 10,000 Homeless*, created by Metro-wide Engagement on Shelter and Housing (MESH), a partnership between counties and nonprofits to address the need and root causes of homelessness. Catholic Charities of St. Paul and Minneapolis is also a leader in working to foster a critical awareness of social issues for their volunteers. They provided our group with a tour and explanation of the site's operations before the serving of the meals, and followed the experience with an onsite reflection and interactive debriefing.

Final Projects and Evaluation

The final assignment applied what they learned in a project that would enhance their understanding of the course content, improve their teaching practice, or entail a relevant action-research project. The projects were impressive and varied, including action research on gender stereotyping in fifth and sixth grade and facilitating cultural awareness in a homogenous classroom. Examples of curriculum development projects were "What We Don't Know about Race Does Hurt Us: A Curriculum for High School Biology," "Sweatshop and Globalization Unit for High School Advanced Algebra?"

and "Social Justice and Curriculum Integration: Using Online Discussion Forum in High School English." Some students participated in community forums and workshops, such as Mirrors of Privilege: Making Whiteness Visible and Racial Bias in the Classroom, conducted by Shakti Butler, and Whiteness and Hurricane Katrina, conducted by Tim Wise.

They were an interesting, hardworking group of teachers who raised great questions and contributed thoughtfully to discussion. As in any classroom, the students were all at different stages in their ability to view the world and education critically; but, throughout the course, their discussion, writing, and practice demonstrated that they all progressed to more complex understandings and a greater commitment to educational praxis for social justice.

CHAPTER EIGHT

Program Development: Strategies for Building and Sustaining Your Service-Learning Program

Service-learning has to do with powerful purposes—getting kids into the world. Jean Piaget says schooling isn't worth anything unless it creates for people the capacity to believe that when they leave school, they can change the world. If our kids don't believe they can change the world, then I think we ought to say that our education has not been powerful enough.

—Vito Perrone, Harvard Graduate School of Education[1]

Program Foundation and Design

With considerable time and energy expended in building effective service-learning experiences and programs in K–12 schools and higher education, how can we ensure program longevity in spite of personnel changes and budget cuts? There are no guarantees, but there are strategies that schools and colleges can implement to assist them in overcoming obstacles, increasing the likelihood that their service-learning programs will thrive and endure.

Mission and History

Building an enduring social-justice service-learning program requires a solid foundation. Examining the school's mission and history for evidence of commitment to service and civic engagement is an important first step. Even if the word *service* is not specifically stated in the mission statement, educational institutions often include goals—related to citizenship, critical thinking, community connection, and values such as justice, equality, and respect for diversity—that can be achieved through service-learning.

You can research the origin and history of your institution to find traditions of service to the community, collaboration with social and political causes for the betterment of society, and work for the advancement of democratic ideals. Prominent teachers, administrators, and benefactors who were and are committed to and engaged in community service can be inspirational models for advancing the program.

When teachers and administrators connect the social-justice service-learning program to the mission and tradition of the institution, it embodies a greater purpose. Service-learning becomes a strategy to help fulfill the mission and reach educational goals and outcomes. As service-learning becomes more widespread in the institution, faculty, students, alumni, and parents become more aware of the benefits and see it as part of the fiber of the school community.

Service Program Design

A multifocal service-learning program can foster a culture of service in an institution. Service can be organized by courses or integrated into academic departments and extracurricular clubs and activities. Additionally, there may be campuswide service-learning experiences organized by the institution. Examining Benilde–St. Margaret's (BSM) program design provides concrete examples of design features that can be adapted to meet the needs of other educational settings.

Service Courses

Service classes in theology provide students opportunities to reflect on their values and beliefs and have conversations on important issues, such as the meaning of living a moral, ethical life. All students are required to take a religion class with a Catholic social-teaching component. Using *Catholic Social Teachings*[2] as a foundational text, students are encouraged to examine current societal values and create an alternative vision for a society based on social justice. Students affirm the value of each person and come to regard themselves as a part of something larger, connected to others outside of their immediate community.

Teachers encourage students to volunteer with agencies serving marginalized populations, most frequently people living in poverty or people living with mental or physical challenges. Having a service experience embedded in a semester class allows adequate preparation before the experience as well as reflection and research during and after the service. Time is devoted to *inward reflection*, asking what effects the experiences had on students, and *outward reflection*, asking why the situation exists and how our actions work for change. As students begin to see the inequities and injustices that exist in the world, service-learning provides them a vehicle to act on their beliefs and make a difference.

Students select from among several courses:

The Christian Service course centers on student volunteers working in the community. Three hours of service work are required per week, for a total of sixty hours. Students explore connections between Catholic social teachings and their service work. This class gives students the opportunity to stretch their knowledge of the world, meet new people, and see that faith involves service, commitment, and intellectual understanding.

In the Service Leadership course, students study many historical and current religious leaders to learn about different leadership styles and discern the most effective styles for themselves. Students apply what they have learned about themselves as leaders in the design and implementation of service projects in the community. Two important components driving the success of these projects are students recruiting other students to help, and securing necessary resources from businesses or donors. A minimum of thirty service hours is required.

The Social Justice and Nonviolence course focuses on the role of the Catholic Church in the modern global society. Students examine recent Church documents, especially documents relating to Catholic social teachings, and research nonprofit organizations with social-justice missions; and they prepare a peace and justice fair for members of the school community.

La Religion, Cultura, y Justicia en America Latina is a bilingual course that deepens students' understanding of Catholic social teachings in the context of the Latin American struggle for justice. Students learn about Latin Americans and personalize the importance of connecting cultural and religious ideas to social change. Students and teachers have developed an ongoing relationship with Los Pequeños Hermanos in Guatemala, and several participate in a two-week summer mission trip to work with their community.[3]

Sample student-initiated projects have included creating Hmong intergenerational cultural workshops for teens to learn about language and culture from the elders; converting a storage space into a children's playroom at Interfaith Hospitality Homeless Shelter; writing and creating a children's photo-journal explaining what will happen during their stay at Children's Hospital for heart surgery; and teaching art, acting, reading, and cheerleading classes at day-care and after-school care centers serving families living in poverty.

Service in Other Academic Departments

Individual teachers in academic departments such as science, world language, English, social studies, fine arts, and mathematics integrate service-learning experiences into their curriculum. A sampling of these projects follows.

Science teachers and students have been involved in a variety of environmental projects. In conjunction with the City of St. Louis Park, the Minnesota Department of Natural Resources, and the University of Minnesota, students addressed issues of buckthorn eradication, purple-loosestrife control, and neighborhood environmental education. Ecology students worked with the Minnehaha Creek Watershed Project and conducted water-quality testing in Twin Lakes, on city property adjacent to our school. Other science students participated in a joint Eyes on Wild Life and Minnesota Department of Natural Resources project to capture, collar, and release deer and timberwolves in northern Minnesota.

Many students in the senior government course volunteer as election judges at voting sites. Art students make and donate ceramic bowls for the city's Hungry Bowls benefit luncheon. Geography students have studied global-hunger issues and volunteered at a food-distribution agency sending meals to Haiti. Math students tutor in after-school programs.

Service Through Extracurricular Activities

Students, coaches, and advisers continue their service commitment through many clubs, groups, and teams, such as Red Knight Volunteer Corps, Peers Respecting Others, peer ministers, mission trips, Red Carpet Club, athletic and activities teams, National Honor Society, and student council. While not all activities are service-learning experiences, they meet real needs in the community and contribute to creating an ethic of service. Below are some noteworthy examples occurring over the last decade.

The Red Knight Volunteer Corps program began as an opportunity for junior-high students to volunteer. The initial club of twenty-five students quickly grew and expanded to freshmen and sophomores and then, as students became upperclassmen, they continued as senior advisers. The students have set up an organizational system of service pods, with older students responsible for the design and implementation of service projects and the documentation of service hours. This club, which began as a means to expose younger students to service, has become a critical service force in the community. Human service agencies, education programs, and volunteer agencies contact BSM for ready volunteers when they have a need. The effects of this club have been expanded services in the community, increased student training, and a dramatic increase in Presidential Service Awards. In 2008, 96 high-school students received the Presidential Volunteer Service Award for contributing at least one hundred hours of service in twelve months, as did 7 junior-high students, for serving at least fifty hours—totaling 13,702 hours for these 103 volunteers.

Students in BSM's diversity club have organized a series of activities for the entire school to highlight diverse perspectives and cultures, which have included presentations on Jewish holidays and Kwanzaa and a Native American powwow, as well as a diversity film-and-discussion series. Students have cofacilitated workshops on race, class, and gender for each grade level, and they helped design and conduct a collaborative student diversity conference for area independent schools' students and teachers.

Student leaders in National Honor Society and student council have organized several service projects including school blood drives, Christmas baskets, and a senior citizen's prom. Red Carpet Club students serve as tour guides at open houses for prospective students and host visiting students for a day. Peer ministers are trained as leaders for freshman and sophomore retreats. The band, choir, and orchestra have performed at schools, churches, and nursing homes. They have also provided music for the National Catholic Educational Association Conference and have been guest musicians at state and national workshops.

With a multifocal approach to service-learning, students grow with service as an integral part of their lives. As discussed earlier, students continue to serve as they leave the BSM community and carry the ethic of service into other communities.

Building and Sustaining a Service-Learning Program

In addition to building the service-learning foundation on the school's mission and traditions and integrating it through various courses and clubs, there are seven key areas that contribute to the growth and sustainability of service-learning programs: garnering and growing support, policy changes, funding and awards, faculty development, the service coordinator role, student leadership development, and partnership development.[4] As we walk through these topics using BSM's experiences as examples, it is interesting to note that programs and institutions, like individuals, move through stages of development. Chapter 9 explores the critical-consciousness development of an institution.

Garnering and Growing Support

Having a broad support base is vital to advancing your program. The first phase is what I call "the hook." How do we get groups excited about service-learning and garner initial support? Then, how do we integrate service practices and keep the momentum growing? When identifying different audiences, teachers or administrators analyze and select approaches that click with their individual and collective interests.

Administration

For administrators and board members, effective marketing is the hook. Target their current goals and show how service-learning can be a powerful tool to achieve them. Our key issues were student academic achievement and character development, so we presented research on how service-learning improves student learning. Similar to most top administrators, our president was always looking for ways to build school pride and community relations, and he understood that good public relations are priceless.

Faculty and Staff

Initially, use student voices and stories to pique teacher interest. Reading student reflections on their service experiences or a letter from an agency at a faculty meeting is very powerful. Another hook is to invite individuals or several teachers within a department to participate in one-time service opportunities. This provides them with a nonthreatening, collegial experience in which they feel good about volunteering and contributing to the community, and it helps them better understand students' service experience. After the event, word-of-mouth marketing engenders positive attitudes and increases the desire of others to volunteer. Administrators or colleagues can also highlight specific projects that teachers are doing in the classroom, planting seeds for additional projects.

One of the most powerful hooks for teachers is seeing the impact service-learning has in their courses. The service-learning coordinator makes the case for incorporating service-learning by explaining how these experiences increase the value and meaning of a class and help students make real-life connections to the curriculum.

Students and Parents

Sparking interest in students is easy. The idea of doing something different outside of the classroom, where they can be active, apply what they know, and learn at the same time, is engaging. Their experiences are powerful and empowering. Parents become attracted to service-learning because of its potential to impact their children in terms of personal growth, character development, and career exploration.

Community Partners

Initial relationship building with community and nonprofit agencies, neighboring schools, senior-citizens centers, hospitals, and other sites is very important. Strategies include making the first call and reaching out to the agency staff member, teacher, or volunteer coordinator, and working with that person to identify meaningful work that fills a real need. Then, the key to a maintaining a good partnership is to prepare the students well, have ongoing communication, and request feedback from the site coordinator. Poorly prepared students can create more work for an often already overworked and underfunded agency.

Policy Changes

As the service-learning program develops and evolves, teachers and administrators make decisions that result in policy changes to promote, enhance, and eventually sustain a high level of service-learning. These modifications can affect both official and unofficial procedures and policies.

Strategic Leadership

As the saying goes, "Every cause needs a leader." While it's true that one person can start the ball rolling, building and sustaining a program requires many levels of support and leadership. Top-level administrators can set the vision and advocate for a culture that encourages and supports social-justice service-learning. In naming school values, they create the expectation that those ideals will be built into the culture. For example, including social-justice and service experience in the application and interview process, as well as annual goals and performance reviews, presents a strong statement of community values and expectations. Department chairs can also facilitate faculty members' participation in service-learning workshops and provide funding for curriculum development.

Equally important is having a core group of people with a vision and a shared commitment to advancing service-learning programs and sustaining momentum. These are the individuals who meet regularly to discuss the questions, Where are we? Where are we going? and What are the next steps? At BSM, the service-learning coordinator, faith-formation director, and assistant to the president focused on the macro level of institutional change. The motto was "Start small, make it good, and keep moving forward."

For social-justice service-learning to become integrated into the culture and practice of the institution, you need participation at the grassroots level. Service-learning practitioners focus on the micro level of curriculum design and classroom implementation. They talk to colleagues about their successes and failures and mentor other educators who are interested in adding a service component to their courses.

Service-Learning Coordinator Position

Making the commitment to have a full-time service-learning coordinator is a bold statement by the school administrators that they value service-learning and are willing to commit financial resources to create and support the program. Although some schools begin with a part-time coordinator, to be most effective this position cannot just be an add-on to someone's existing duties. Funding a service-learning coordinator position is key to formalizing and growing the program. This person builds the relationships with the community agencies, sets up transportation, helps the teachers with curriculum development, creates opportunities, and coordinates the program. It facilitates and increases the likelihood of participation and success.

Including Service-Learning in School Documents

Another practical strategy is to include social justice and service-learning deliberately in school documents, such as the mission statement, belief statements, and educational goals, as well as the strategic and diversity plans. This act increases the legitimacy of the program and ensures continuation even with changes in faculty, administrators, or board members. These steps create greater public awareness and acknowledgment and build in accountability for developing and sustaining the program. When service-learning is included in the institution's strategic plan and adopted by the board of trustees, funding becomes a higher priority.

Connecting Service-Learning to Other School Initiatives

When educators regard service-learning as a strategy for achieving educational goals and initiatives, it becomes a tool rather than one more thing added to a teacher's plate. Teaching is a wonderful but very demanding field, and there are constantly new skills, mandates, and dispositions that teachers are required to include in the curriculum. By connecting service-learning to these initiatives, teachers can address several issues at once, saving money, effort, and time. For example, when BSM was converting to a social-justice service-learning model, we worked to integrate other school initiatives such as Catholic identity, higher-order thinking skills, technology skills, and multicultural education into the service experiences. A well-designed service-learning project taps into these skills.

Requiring a Service Course for Graduation

Requiring service experiences for graduation is becoming more widespread in high schools and colleges. Being aware of the standards of effective service-learning practices and the vital role reflection plays in learning and critical-consciousness development builds a strong case for service requirements to be fulfilled in the context of service courses, rather than simply requiring a certain number of service hours for graduation. In order for students to have adequate preparation, opportunities for reflection, and support in their critical awakening, they need to have their service experiences in the context of a class. Service embedded in a course with a knowledgeable teacher who facilitates reflection and learning is the optimal situation. Requiring hours without the benefit of a course can present an unfair burden to service agencies and personnel who may need to monitor reluctant students.

Documenting of Service Hours on Transcripts

Creating and maintaining a record of student service not only demonstrates the value the institution places on service, but also collects data on individual and program outcomes. Documenting student service hours on transcripts provides verification and recognition of students and their contributions to the community. It can also present a broader picture of students' learning experiences and commitment when they are applying to educational programs or seeking employment.

At BSM we have a manageable, fairly simple system to collect and document service hours, using a matrix of the school's educational outcomes and a three-point scale indicating to what extent students exercised those skills during a particular service activity. Students who want service hours documented on their transcripts complete the form, reflect on their service projects, and have the supervisor or teacher sign it. The service-learning coordinator verifies the signature, a student worker enters the approved number of hours on a spreadsheet, and a label with the total hours is put on the student's transcript.

Funding and Awards

Receiving awards and grants is a major catalyst in creating, nurturing, and sustaining service-learning programs. Having a central person, such as the service-learning coordinator, who knows the history and culture of the school and is knowledgeable about curriculum development, educational programs, and evaluation can be effective in grant writing. Successful awards and grants demonstrate the school's ability to deliver on the granting agency's priorities and opens doors to other opportunities. Incorporating a service component into other grants projects often enhances the proposal, making it more attractive. A solid first proposal, in which philosophy, mission, objectives, timetables, evaluation plan, and examples and evidence of service and student activities are well articulated, becomes a template for additional grant and award opportunities.

BSM applied for and received grants, which made it possible to pay expenses for professional development, conference expenses, guest speakers, and materials. We offered teacher stipends for workshop attendance, curriculum design, and project development, as well as expenses for project implementation. By the time the grant period ended, service-learning had become a core program with such strong support from the community that the school added a $10,000 line item to the budget.

Faculty-Development Model for Service-Learning

Professional development is critical in order to convert from community service to service-learning, and then to a social-justice service-learning program. An effective training-program model begins with building awareness of service-learning and providing educators with opportunities to engage in service. As interest builds, schools provide teacher workshops making the case for incorporating service-learning, instruction on the major concepts of service-learning, and necessary tools for initiating a service program.

Offering opportunities for large- and small-group training and incorporating student presentations and reflections were effective in garnering teacher support and participation. Initial exposure and general presentations were given to the entire faculty, followed by discipline-specific and more detailed work sessions for those teachers electing to participate. Having funding to support teacher time for workshops outside the school day, curriculum development stipends, and recognition for efforts and accomplishments fosters participation and success. For example, these are the professional development steps we took:

1. The service-learning coordinator began with awareness building at faculty meetings, giving a ten-minute presentation on specific student

projects. Hearing students speak or read excerpts from their reflections was extremely powerful. We followed up with articles and opportunities for interested teachers.

2. The service-learning coordinator offered groups of teachers exposure to service opportunities such as food shelves, soup kitchens, and tutoring with second-language learners. These were one-time or ongoing projects on a "come when you can" basis.

3. The service-learning coordinator offered workshops on the value and potential of service-learning, as well as presentations that connected it to other school initiatives, such as a presentation on service-learning and multicultural education.

4. Workshops were tailored directly to the needs of a particular department or group. For example, twenty-five teachers elected to participate in eight hours of environmental service-learning training, and the world language department worked with a curriculum specialist to identify potential service-learning projects that dovetailed with its curriculum.

5. After three years, the service-learning coordinator recognized the need for differentiated training for beginning and experienced teachers. Through growth and attrition, there was a substantial population of new staff members in need of the initial training, while the veteran staff were ready for more advanced training to deepen the service-learning experience. Service-Learning 101 and 102 were developed and offered.

6. One-on-one mentoring contributed to expanding and improving the service-learning program. The service-learning coordinator worked with teachers on initial projects and with those wanting to improve student experiences and learning. In addition, as the body of service-learning practitioners expanded, they helped other teachers in their departments design projects.

Service-Learning Coordinator Role

The service-learning coordinator is the number one resource for teachers to bring service into the classroom. In addition to making the contacts and helping teachers with curriculum and project design, coordination at the building level is also an important responsibility. The service-learning coordinator works as a clearinghouse to monitor and coordinate service activities, to ensure that there are a variety of opportunities throughout the school year and that the quality and integrity of the service-learning program are maintained and supported.

An additional benefit to having a service-learning coordinator on staff is that it enhances the school's potential to receive grants. This position demonstrates the school's commitment to service-learning and the ability to accomplish the tasks outlined in grant proposals.

What does a service-learning coordinator do? Fundamentally, the coordinator is the central person who promotes service-learning and brings continuity to the program. Without a service-learning coordinator, we could not have institutionalized our program. We knew we could have spectacular projects, but realized it would not be sustainable. If the teacher left, so would the projects. The service-learning coordinator will

- build and sustain partnerships in the community;
- provide support and coordination for all aspects of schoolwide projects;
- plan and be responsible for the practical nuts and bolts of projects;
- troubleshoot when things do not go according to plan;
- provide educational and service resources to teachers, students, and parents;
- monitor students' work at various agencies;
- assist classroom teachers with logistics such as phone calls, bussing, scheduling, chaperoning, and follow-through;
- monitor documentation of service hours;
- plan and assist in faculty development;
- respond to numerous requests for volunteers in the community by connecting students with community needs.

Student-Leadership Development

One of the key components in service-learning is student leadership. As students engage in service-learning, they gain positive leadership skills. They grow in confidence when they see themselves as useful members of the wider community who are empowered to make a difference. When students are faced with the grim reality of poverty, injustice, and political and economic problems in the news, they can feel helpless, angry, or cynical, and service-learning gives students a vehicle to make positive change.

In service classes, students learn life skills. It is amazing to see students who are technologically advanced with computers, text-messaging, blogging, and social networking but afraid to make a call to an agency and explain what they are interested in doing. With support and practice, they overcome their anxiety.

Here are a few examples that demonstrate student-leadership skills development in BSM students. During a construction project in 1999, science students worked with a landscape architect to design the layout of the school grounds, then presented the drawings to the school board building committee. The board was very impressed with their knowledge and presentation. More recently, junior-high students researched the benefits of a green school and presented a convincing PowerPoint presentation to the school building committee, arguing for environmental change.

Often students would begin to volunteer at a particular site and then become aware of a particular need. In the context of class discussions and brainstorming they would assess what was going wrong, devise a plan, and recruit friends to help implement the projects:

- A student volunteering in a community center in a high-poverty area noticed that the game room was uninviting, had no games, and needed painting. She started collecting children's books and toys and recruited other students and teachers to help paint the room and sand and varnish the floor, and she painted a mural on the wall.
- After volunteering at Nuestros Pequeños Hermanos orphanage in Guatemala, two senior girls returned with a mission to continue to support the children and teachers, and successfully procured over $17,000 in school supplies and donations.
- Students would often begin providing service as part of a service class and then roll their projects over to their extracurricular activities. Working in an infant day-care and after-school center serving low-income families as part of their course experiences, several students developed an annual "baby-shower drive" to furnish supplies and equipment to the center.
- Students often took the lead in convincing additional teachers to include service-learning in their classes. In one case, students asked their math teacher why students in the other teacher's sections tutored at a neighboring elementary school, and expressed a desire to do so as well. Their motivation convinced their math teacher to contact the service-learning coordinator and incorporate service-learning.

Partnership Development

Developing relationships with a variety of agencies, youth groups, and schools is vital to building an effective service-learning program. The service-learning coordinator works with agencies to match appropriate students with the needs of the service sites. The partnership is a two-way relationship, both giving and receiving. Being aware that the students and the school benefit from the service opportunities, it is important to ensure that the needs of the agency are being met as well.

As part of preservice preparation, students learn about the people they will serve and their circumstances. Teachers must be direct in conveying to the students that, yes, they are helping the agency, but the agency is also providing a learning opportunity for them, and they have a responsibility to the agency.

One of the lessons the service-learning coordinator at BSM learned about partnership development was to start with a small project, make it good, and let it grow. She was working with a senior-citizen center that was reluctant to have junior-high students serve meals at the center. The service-learning coordinator worked with their volunteer coordinator and convinced her to try it once. The center was so impressed with the junior-high students' kindness and responsibility that they continue to call on our students whenever they have special events.

The service-learning coordinator developed additional strategies over time to find and develop successful partnerships:

- Have students help research opportunities through their neighborhoods, religious establishments, and organizations.
- Make visits to agencies, and select kid-friendly sites that support the learning aspect of service-learning as well.
- Take tours with students so they have choices and see possibilities.
- Begin with a one-time project and let it grow.
- Have an open relationship with agencies and request feedback.
- Make sure agencies understand the "what" and "why" behind the students' service.
- Show appreciation to agencies for allowing students the opportunity to serve.
- Set clear expectations for students' behaviors and attitudes and hold them accountable.

Creating a Culture of Service

As teachers and students develop a critical stance on service-learning, we have seen how their orientation to service-learning moves from charity to caring to social justice. An important part of building and sustaining a social-justice service-learning program is creating a culture of service throughout the school community. Using our experiences at BSM as a case study provides useful examples.

In 1996 we began to formalize and promote a service-learning program. After three years, when we applied to the National Service-Learning Leader

School Award, given by the Corporation for National Service, our application correctly stated,

> Service is coordinated and well integrated into the life of the school. Service is a part of who we are as demonstrated by our history, our climate and supportive structures, and by the numbers of individuals involved. Students, faculty, parents, and alumni all participate in service. It is included in our mission, belief statements, and educational outcomes, diversity plan, and Strategic Plan 1997–2002. Serving is an ethic at Benilde-St. Margaret's School.

How did this culture of service happen? During those three years we created our reality. We simply began to talk about service as an important part of our tradition, our mission, and our future.

We kept service on the front page, and it became how we defined ourselves. We were deliberate in highlighting the service work of students and teachers. Our student and community newspapers, alumni publications, and monthly parent packet all consistently recounted service stories, such as ecology students conducting water testing for the State Department, French students raising funds for a teacher's salary in Haiti, or a student collecting seventy-five boxes of books for a community center's library in a low-income area.

We recognized and honored parents for their extensive service to the school community. They provide direct services to the school by staffing the student career center, welcoming new parents, and promoting a student-recognition program. Parents also host community building and fundraising events, as well as supporting athletics and activities events. Additionally, they organize and support educational workshops and speaker programs for parents and students.

While we were talking the talk, we were also walking the walk, implementing teacher training and capacity building for integrated, effective service projects. During these three years, in addition to regularly scheduled faculty in-services, twenty teachers attended state or national service-learning conferences. Furthermore, twenty-three teachers voluntarily attended eight hours of service-learning training in the evenings. The interest and momentum continued to grow.

Last and most importantly, we gave students the freedom and support to think big and do great things. We were overwhelmed with the breadth and depth of the projects they designed and implemented to meet real needs in the community. They were committed and resourceful, and while projects did not always follow their intended plans and timelines, the students had great learning experiences.

Looking back, a major factor in keeping us focused and always moving forward was documentation and accountability. From 1997, when we first applied for the grant, through 2003, we were required to submit quarterly progress reports to the state. Our three core people consistently met, discussed, and documented progress. We also assessed the program and regularly set new goals.

In January 2003, we administered a faculty survey to measure the level of teacher support, knowledge, and experience with service. Thirty-six percent of the teachers reported a very good or excellent understanding, and another third had a good understanding of service-learning. Almost 70 percent had attended a workshop or training session, and 50 percent had implemented at least one service-learning project in their courses. The survey also indicated that 100 percent of the teachers volunteered personally or professionally in their communities, their places of worship, or the school community, or in professional organizations. Half of the faculty engaged in service regularly, and another 35 percent were extensively involved. The overall survey findings indicated that there was strong, broad-based support for service-learning as a learning strategy, and that teachers were committed to and modeled service.

As far as we have come, without focused attention and nurturing, programs can falter and lose ground. We need to acknowledge the challenges and learn to expect the unexpected. We found that by embracing mistakes as learning opportunities, we can build on what we have learned for the future.

We did and do still have challenges. A teacher would conduct a great service-learning project for a few years, and then, because of schedule changes, a newly assigned teacher would be too busy learning the curriculum to continue the project. Often there is a change of personnel or priorities in a service agency, and we lose a great site. For several years, two teachers accompanied ten seniors to Guatemala to lay cement slabs and build homes with and for Guatemalan families. The organization decided to work more with churches and families, and our ten-year connection ended.

"Life happens" (babies, illness, relocations), and new time commitments and priorities (family needs, study for advanced degrees, new opportunities) arise. There are bound to be dips and upswings in enthusiasm and program outcomes; but starting with a solid foundation, building capacity, and maintaining a habit of continuous improvement help in addressing program needs and making adjustments along the way. Once there is a critical mass of around 20 percent, the momentum is in place to continue growth. I return to our mantra: "Start small, make it good, and keep moving forward."

For educators and institutions interested in building service-learning programs that generate experiences, attitudes, and behaviors leading to a committed citizenry engaged in service for positive social change, I offer these suggestions:

- Incorporate civic engagement and a commitment to social justice in the school's educational vision and mission. Promoting practices that are aligned with, and developing a culture that is committed to, core democratic principles such as equality, justice, and pluralism will provide the basis for critical multiculturalism, as well as moral and civic education. Parks[5] and Colby and others.[6] provide solid background on mentoring institutions and moral and civic education.

- Integrate the service experiences into courses. This is essential for promoting an understanding of populations served and social issues such as poverty, homelessness, racism, oppression, and sociopolitical economic hegemony. Likewise, critical reflection should be integrated before, during, and after the service experience and must include both inward reflection (values, racial-identity formation, internalized racism, sexism, classism, White privilege) and outward reflection (society as it is and could be, systems of oppression, power relations, class structure, social reproduction). Students need to be active subjects in creating their own view of the world, which can be accomplished by incorporating discussion and reflection strategies, such as problem posing, perspective taking, critical narratives, films, and independent research.

- Develop partnerships with agencies and community groups committed to social justice that facilitate students' interactions with people living in poverty and people from other ethnic and racial groups. In working with agencies that not only address immediate needs, but also work for long-term solutions and political change, students meet other adults committed to social change, gain advocacy skills, and see new avenues to effect change.

- Design opportunities for students to serve with their peers and/or family members. This deepens the experience and reinforces the ethic of service. It is also important to include the informational and reflection components in organized family service experiences.

- Include student study and service opportunities abroad. This is a powerful tool with the potential for dramatic growth in critical-consciousness development. I direct educators to the insightful research of Kiely for further elaboration on international service learning.[7]

If your service-learning program is to be successful, thriving, and enduring, you need to be intentional in its design and operation. Integrating the ethic of service into your school's mission, curriculum design, and requirements, as well as providing budgetary and personnel support, are important factors. Another element to consider as you prepare for this journey is that just as individuals advance through stages of critical-consciousness development, so will your institution. In chapter 9, we will explore the stages of institutional critical-consciousness development.

CHAPTER NINE

Program Development: Continuing the Journey

Stages of Institutional Critical Consciousness

The focus of this book is using service-learning and critical-consciousness development as a path to fostering the emergence of engaged citizens who are committed to working for social justice. Thus far the emphasis has been the stages of individual critical consciousness and programs that support students as they become more critically aware. In a similar manner, we can identify stages of institutional development as the educational community becomes more deeply tied to social-justice action. Students, teachers, administrators, and the institution itself evolve as the orientation to service-learning changes from charity to caring to social justice.

As we have seen, students in the initial charity stage enjoy volunteering because it makes them feel good about themselves. Service is a part of the culture, and everyone is doing it. As they move to the caring stage, students realize that what they do makes a difference to people because they have come to know and care about them. In the social-justice stage, the ethic of service and the commitment to create a more just world are integral to students' identity, and they incorporate these values into their future plans and vocations. How do these changes emerge for teachers and institutions?

Often educators become interested in service-learning because they see other teachers and students involved in projects. At this initial stage, their goal is to use service-learning as a strategy to help them reach course objectives and make their classes more fun and relevant. As teachers become more involved, they see the impact service-learning experiences have on them, as well as on their students and those they serve. The teacher comes to care more deeply and makes a personal and emotional investment in nurturing students, as well as the populations being served.

As educators move to the social-justice stage, there is a fundamental shift in how we view our role as teachers and the goals we have for our students. Teachers are aware of the political nature of education, which may serve to reproduce, resist, and/or transform the status quo. We become colearners with our students as they investigate the causes of social issues, the effects of public policy, and the possibility for change. Education becomes an act of social justice, as educators help young people develop critical skills to understand and improve the world.

We see similar shifts at the institutional level. Often at the charity stage, administrators regard service-learning as a form of positive public relations that will garner community support. Service-learning at this stage is a strategy that achieves many objectives, such as increasing student learning and attendance, improving student behavior, and building leadership skills. The school receives strong support from parents who may see service-learning as an opportunity for their children to explore career options and build self-esteem, while enhancing their profiles for future use in college or job interviews.

When students and teachers expand and deepen their service-learning experiences, the institution becomes more connected to the wider community. Administrators better understand the breadth and depth of community need and change policies to encourage and facilitate addressing those needs through service-learning. As school personnel develop stronger partnerships with community members and agencies, the institution affirms its obligation to contribute to the community and formalizes the commitment. The institution moves beyond the notion that "service-learning is good for the school" to "service-learning is important because we care about and are connected to the community, and we can make a difference."

The institution's movement toward a social-justice orientation to service-learning is fostered by parallel changes in the individuals who comprise and lead the institution. As teachers, students, and administrators become critically aware and engage in service for social change, the institution deepens its commitment to social justice. This is demonstrated through expanding and elevating the service and social-justice components of its mission and providing support for continued development of people and programs.

Evolution of Programs

The preceding chapters have examined strategies to build effective service-learning programs in K–12 schools, a case study of critical-consciousness development in a multicultural course with a service component, and tools for sustaining and institutionalizing service-learning programs. While institutionalizing the program ensures ongoing commitment and longevity, it does not translate into a static program cemented in the past. As the institution's understanding and commitment to justice evolves, so does the program. For instance, Benilde–St. Margaret's School (BSM) has emerging service paths: the Common Basket, servant leadership, and social entrepreneurship.

The Common Basket

The Common Basket program came into being as my colleague, Lisa Lenhart-Murphy, was looking for a way to develop a well-rounded approach to service that included time, talent, and treasure. Students were already deeply involved in, and generous with, sharing their time and talents through service to a wide variety of communities. Now she saw the opportunity to educate students about philanthropy and stewardship and engage them in contributing their treasure.

Working within the faith-formation department, the teachers looked back to the values and traditions of the school's founding orders, the Benedictines, the Sisters of St. Joseph of Carondelet, and the Christian Brothers. The history of all three orders included a strong commitment to service, social justice, and, especially, service to the poor. The teachers recognized the importance of connecting to the school's roots in developing this program, which they found in the Christian Brothers practice of a "common basket."

Historically, the Christian Brothers founded schools for children living in poverty. Over the course of time their schools became noted for providing excellent education, and families who had means wanted to send their children to the brothers' schools. The brothers welcomed the new students and were careful to institute practices ensuring that social and economic differences did not affect the community: they wanted all students to feel equally valued. One such practice was the *common basket*. Each day as the students arrived at school, those who had bread for lunch placed it in a large basket. At lunch the leaders would distribute the food from the common basket to all the children, so that no child was embarrassed or neglected.[1]

Under the guidance of BSM's chaplain, Tim Wozniak, the faith-formation department modeled this approach. In the 2008 fall workshop, the Common

Basket program was introduced to the faculty and staff. During a prayer service, baskets were passed; and, as individuals held them, they symbolically placed the talents they brought to the community into the baskets.

During the school's opening Mass, students passed baskets, and all seventh-through twelfth-graders reflected on their talents. Again in October, during homecoming liturgy, the students symbolically placed in the basket their offerings of time: service time they contributed to the school community, each other, their families, and the broader community. Having reflected on their talents and time, students were given the opportunity during the Thanksgiving liturgy to make financial contributions to a specific cause. Student leaders pass several baskets around the aisles, and all the funds were collected in one large, common basket. Once a month over the next six months, baskets were passed, and students shared their "treasures" by making donations.

Under the social-justice service-learning model, educational connections and reflection were essential components to building an understanding of need, as well as of historical and social-justice issues in the community. Academic departments took on the responsibility of informing their students of the Common Basket initiative for the month, providing reflection activities, and reminding students as the collection date drew near.

Another important aspect of the contributions was that the students needed to reflect on the need and be in solidarity with those who were suffering. This meant contributing money that they had specifically earned and saved, or that they had saved as a result of an active decision to deny themselves something, such as a DVD or going to the movies. It was heartwarming to see junior-high students placing plastic bags of coins in the basket. Building their advocacy skills, students could educate others, such as family members, friends, or neighbors, about the need and solicit donations; but they were encouraged not to just ask for funds from their parents.

When possible, people who were personally touched by a tragedy or were working with a specific need made presentations to the students as part of the educational component. This contributed to students' understanding and moved them from charity to caring, and in some cases to social justice. For example, a young man who worked at Feed My Starving Children explained how the organization had worked with scientists from major food companies in the Twin Cities, such as Cargill and General Mills, to develop a highly nutritious mixture to meet the needs of severely malnourished children. This food, which is easy and safe to transport and is culturally acceptable worldwide, is distributed to the poorest of the poor and has a dramatic impact on the health and lives of children.[2] The amount contributed by the students fed 19,000 children in Haiti.

A faculty member with relatives in a Minnesota rural community described the ravages of flooding in the area and the desperate situations of the people and their town a year later. Students felt connected to the flood victims through her stories. Students were moved to action. First they studied the current situation in Rushford, and increased general awareness through a letter campaign in which they solicited funds. Later that year, the religion classes revived the story, showing the human suffering, and collected funds in the spring common basket.

Through the help of a BSM counselor and his daughter's volunteer experiences, the story of "the lost boys of Sudan" became real when Ting, one of the boys (now a young man), came to school. He repeated his story throughout the day to small groups of students in their social-studies classes. As a result of learning about the situation, understanding on a personal level, and reflecting on their obligation and connection to others, students were moved to action and raised enough money to build a well in the Sudan.

Two junior-high social-studies teachers had traveled to Rwanda to learn about its history and culture and the genocide of 1994. They had talked to many people, and incorporated what they learned into their Genocide and Social Justice class. Again the information became personal to students as they put a face on the tragedy and heard the amazing stories of Rwandan people coming forward to make a difference and reconcile these tragic events.

Throughout the year, the Common Basket program created a sense of solidarity globally and locally, and the students raised over $24,000. The last collection of the year was for the benefit of those people in our own community who needed support and assistance with their tuition. As a reflection activity prior to the collection, teachers randomly asked five students to leave the classroom and stand in the hall, to underscore the need for tuition assistance at our school. Students recognized that everyone is a valued member and the community would be lessened if even one person were missing.

Servant Leadership

Within the past few years, individuals in our community began to talk about servant leadership and the underlying principles characterizing a *servant leader*. As more people learned about this concept, they saw it as a worthy goal. Servant leadership is based on the central message of loving and serving others. By connecting with our Catholic heritage, modeling servant leadership in our interactions, and integrating the values into the curriculum, the community would develop their skills to serve and lead.

Robert Greenleaf, who coined the phrase "servant leadership," popularized the servant model in 1970 in *The Servant as Leader*. Greenleaf describes a servant leader as someone who has a natural desire to serve and makes a conscious choice to lead. Servant leadership makes each individual the primary focus, whereas traditional leadership's primary focus is achieving results.[3]

When leaders of companies such as AT&T and Southwest Airlines embraced this model of leadership and practiced it in their daily lives, their companies' productivity and profits soared. However, as Kent Keith, Greenleaf Center CEO, suggests in *The Case for Servant Leadership*, the paradox of servant leadership is that if you adopt servant leadership as a means to increase financial gains, results will be disappointing. If you become a servant leader to serve others, results flourish.[4]

The ten core principles of a servant leader, as described by Greenleaf, are listening, empathy, healing, awareness, persuasion, vision, foresight, stewardship, commitment to the growth of people, and community building.[5] These principles speak to the hearts and minds of educators who see social justice as core to their vocation and to institutions whose missions include service and social justice.

In 2008, as an initial task in our strategic-planning process at BSM, we revised our mission and vision statements to include the goal of "developing engaged, intelligent servant leaders." Since then, teachers, staff, and administrators have learned more and reflected on how we as individuals and as an institution incorporate the ten servant-leader principles in our daily work. We discussed how we attend to and serve those for whom we are responsible, and also affirm servant leaders in our community.

Zach Zeckser, a religious-education teacher at BSM who had studied servant leadership, was the point person for leading our community in profes-

Table 9.1.   Attitudes and Behaviors of Servant Leaders

- Trust their followers
- Work with their followers
- Have earned respect
- Set the standards by example
- Can see through the eyes of their followers
- Glorify team spirit
- Build up team members and offer a hand
- Have faith in people
- Use their heads but also their hearts
- Dream big and act big
- Help realize their followers' dreams
- Say "let's go!" not "get going!"
- Laugh at themselves
- Have open minds

sional development. In one of his presentations, he described servant leaders' attitudes and corresponding beliefs.[6]

BSM is beginning the journey of becoming a community that lives and teaches the principles of servant leadership. At this point we are still discovering what servant leadership is, the form it will take in our community, and how to embrace and model this leadership style. In addition to discussion and professional development, one concrete step we have taken is to highlight students and adults within our community who embody servant leadership in their work. These profiles are prominently featured on the school's home page.[7]

Social Entrepreneurship

In addition to the Common Basket and servant leadership, we are introducing the concept of *social entrepreneurship* to our students. Social entrepreneurship applies business methods and principles to solving social problems, through innovation, empowerment, and social change. This concept goes beyond the charity-justice debate by changing the terrain. Philanthropy and charity combine with business interests to achieve goals that both improve society and promote economic development.

Throughout history, many individuals have recognized a social problem left unaddressed by the community, government, or business, and, through creative problem solving and risk taking, found new solutions. People like Jane Addams, who in the 1880s created the Hull House—a settlement house in Chicago to improve immigrants' living situation—or Vinoba Bhave, who started the Bhoodan, or Land Gift, movement in 1951 to redistribute land to India's poor are classic examples of social entrepreneurs.

A more contemporary example is Muhammad Yunus. A banker and economist, Yunus developed the concept of *microcredit* in the 1970s and gave loans to entrepreneurs in Bangladesh who were too poor to qualify. He found that making small loan to individuals enabled them to start businesses, become self-sufficient, and repay the loans, resulting in social and economic development in the community. Yunus and Grameen Bank were awarded the Nobel Peace Prize in 2006. Today several foundations and organizations exist to support and advance social and economic development through social entrepreneurship.

Behind one of these is Bill Drayton, who founded Ashoka, a global nonprofit dedicated to helping social entrepreneurs succeed. He describes social entrepreneurs as "individuals with innovative solutions to society's most pressing social problems. They are ambitious and persistent, tackling major social issues and offering new ideas for wide-scale change." Ashoka's vision and mission communicate the organization's position and commitment to social change:

> Vision: Ashoka envisions an Everyone A Changemaker™ world. A world that responds quickly and effectively to social challenges, and where each individual has the freedom, confidence and societal support to address any social problem and drive change.
>
> Mission: Ashoka strives to shape a global, entrepreneurial, competitive citizen sector: one that allows social entrepreneurs to thrive and enables the world's citizens to think and act as changemakers.[8]

Ashoka has supported over 2,000 social entrepreneurs in over sixty countries in realizing social change through programs in education, health, environment, human rights, economic development, and civic engagement.

Another concrete example of a social entrepreneur is Jeff Skoll. In 1996, as president and the first full-time employee of eBay, Skoll was instrumental in creating the eBay Foundation, based on the philosophy of empowerment; and in 1999 he created the Skoll foundation, which "drives large-scale change by investing in, connecting, and celebrating social entrepreneurs and other innovators dedicated to solving the world's most pressing problems."

Defining a *change agent* as a "pioneer of innovations that benefit humanity," the Skoll Foundation defines social entrepreneurs as

> the change agents for society, seizing opportunities others miss and improving systems, inventing new approaches and creating sustainable solutions to change society for the better. However, unlike business entrepreneurs who are motivated by profits, social entrepreneurs are motivated to improve society.[9]

In addition to his foundation, Skoll founded Participant Media in 2004, with the belief that "a good story well told can truly make a difference in how one sees the world."[10] Participant Media produces films and documentaries that raise awareness of social issues and develops social-action campaigns that engage viewers to become involved. Among the highly acclaimed films are *An Inconvenient Truth*, *North Country*, and *Good Night and Good Luck*.

Another significant model of social entrepreneurship is the team of Matt and Jessica Flannery, who in 2005 founded Kiva, a nonprofit organization whose mission is "to connect people through lending for the sake of alleviating poverty." Kiva, the first online global microlending organization, connects individual lenders directly to entrepreneurs around the world. Kiva provides the structure for ordinary people to engage in social change by "lend[ing] to a specific entrepreneur, empowering them to lift themselves out of poverty."

Individuals may browse profiles of entrepreneurs on the site and select the people and project they want to help by making a loan. Lenders receive e-mail journals and loan repayment reports. When the loan is repaid, lenders select another entrepreneur and relend the money. Microfinancing reaches real people and enables them to improve their standard of living as well as their communities. Some interesting Kiva facts from November 2009 include the following:

- Total value of all loans made through Kiva: $103,929,135
- Number of Kiva Lenders: 598,710
- Number of countries represented by Kiva Lenders: 187
- Number of entrepreneurs that have received a loan through Kiva: 259,815
- Number of loans that have been funded through Kiva: 148,393
- Percentage of Kiva loans made to women entrepreneurs: 82.59%
- Number of Kiva Field Partners (microfinance institutions Kiva partners with): 106
- Number of countries Kiva Field Partners are located in: 49
- Current repayment rate (all partners): 98.04%
- Average loan size (This is the average amount loaned to an individual Kiva Entrepreneur. Some loans—group loans—are divided between a group of borrowers.): $403.22
- Average total amount per Kiva Lender (with reloaned funds): $174.11
- Average number of loans per Kiva Lender: 5.00[11]

In addition to individual lenders, Kiva's mission and operations are supported by many corporate partners, such as PayPal, Google, American Express, Microsoft, and YouTube. Likewise, they receive institutional support from the W.K. Kellogg Foundation, the Rockefeller Foundation, the Skoll Foundation, and the Clinton Global Initiative.[12]

Increasingly, youth are engaging in social entrepreneurship to address social issues with creative solutions. Matt and Jessica Flannery were in their twenties when they started Kiva. Universities such as New York University, Stanford, and Babson are offering programs in social entrepreneurship. Learn and Serve America's website provides several links to organizations and resources for youth interested in developing entrepreneurial skills to create social change.

In 2009, as part of the Common Basket project at BSM, students were introduced to Kiva and the concept of microlending through their math classes.

As the students and teachers explored the many business initiatives at Kiva, they will also investigate the history and economic development of each country and learned about the relationship between international, community, and individual economic and social development. Students chose which projects to support with loans and will continue to manage the accounts. They will also make decisions on potential service projects that they can connect to their social issue, to expand their opportunities to make a difference.

Engaging Students in the Process

In reflecting on the evolution of our service program by means of its expansion into philanthropy through the Common Basket, servant leadership, and social entrepreneurship, we anticipate deepening the long-term effects of students' commitment to service and action for social justice. In schools and universities, adults can model and help foster a culture of service, but the students are the ones who will sustain the momentum. Over time, we have realized that simply adding more opportunities and activities is not the answer. To achieve sustainable results, we need to be intentional in designing programs, incorporate research-based strategies for high-quality practices, and create an environment where students are internally motivated.

Lenhart-Murphy, BSM's service-learning coordinator, identifies ten attributes that educators need to continuously monitor as their service programs expand and evolve in new directions. The service experience should

- be informational because students need to feel informed and knowledgeable;
- make a link to the curriculum by bringing the issue into the classroom;
- be personal and relevant to the students, which will increase its meaning;
- be meaningful so it becomes a chance for students to act on their beliefs;
- create a deeper understanding of the issues by including the perspective of others;
- create a caring sense of connection by inviting students to be in solidarity with those who struggle;
- involve reflection and provoke students to think critically;
- be voluntary and yet inspire students to participate;
- include student voice and choice;
- be of sufficient length and intensity to develop a long-term commitment to giving.[13]

The reward will be teenagers and young adults who are invested and engaged in local and global communities and empowered to make change in the world. Young people feel valued and needed and find relevance by connecting their learning and lives to real-life situations.[14]

Conclusion

Early service experiences impact adult behavior and attitudes toward service and social justice by fostering a critical consciousness—developing a deeper awareness of self and a deeper awareness and broader perspective of others and social issues, and seeing one's potential to make change. However, experiences in service alone will not generate a commitment to social justice. To accomplish this goal, we need to be intentional in the mission and design of the service program and critically aware of ourselves, in order to guide students in developing a more critical consciousness. There must be a solid grounding in three areas: the institution, the educator, and the student.

At the institutional level, the school's mission and vision should commit to developing moral citizens who will actively engage in the community for the common good. With clarity of purpose, administrators will work to ensure that faculty members share the school's vision and are prepared to implement it. School leaders and educators should be intentional in designing learning opportunities and service experiences that align with this mission and have the power to foster growth in critical consciousness in a respectful, safe, hospitable environment. When we promote practices and develop a culture committed to core democratic principles such as equality, justice, and pluralism, we create the foundation for moral and civic education.

As educators, we need a strong sense of self, feelings of efficacy and agency, and a solid grounding in critical multiculturalism if we are to guide students in developing critical consciousness. With our compass pointed toward social justice, we must commit, not only to teach the content area, but also to attend to the intellectual and emotional lives of the students, as well as their civic-mindedness. Paulo Freire's concept of teaching is founded on a deep respect for everyone and a methodology that assists students in their unveiling of the world. Teachers can provide catalysts for growth through dialogue, reflection, and experiences that foster an awakening over time and allow students to come to their own realizations about the world and their role in it.

Creating opportunities for reflection and action in the community for the purposes of developing critical consciousness is a delicate matter that we need to approach with care. While destabilizing one's understanding of the world is a preliminary step in becoming more critical, we have a responsibility to support students as they question the status quo and envision and build a better world. Attending to future possibilities with hope and agency is as important as, if not more important than, discovering past and current injustices. Teaching for social justice is a rewarding but difficult endeavor that should be entered into with respect, responsibility, and humility.

When students are the subjects of the teaching and learning process, rather than the objects, they actively engage in creating their own view of the world. Likewise, when students participate in social-justice education, they need opportunities to clarify their values and build their own understanding of life's meaning and purpose, so they can decide who they want to be and how they want to live. Their developmental challenge as teens and young adults is to build a positive identity, which involves knowing their talents, feeling capable, and having the potential to make a difference. These are foundational elements for students exploring and developing critical consciousness. As students undertake the work of understanding themselves, others, and the world, they need critical-thinking skills and a supportive environment as they reflect inwardly about themselves and outwardly about the world. It is an empowering undertaking for them to increase their self-awareness while they simultaneously gain new perspectives on others and the ever-changing world.

APPENDIX A

Teaching and Learning Resources

At times our responsibilities as teachers seem endless with more expectations placed on our plate each year. Embracing service-learning helps us engage students in meaningful learning activities in their communities, makes our course content more relevant, and helps us achieve our educational goals. While implementing changes in how and what we teach takes time, the good news is there are tremendous, existing resources and strategies that are easily accessible via Internet.

Multicultural Education and Social Justice Online Resources

Rethinking our Schools
www.rethinkingschools.org

Rethinking Schools is an organization firmly committed to equity and the vision that public education is central to the creation of a humane, caring, multiracial democracy. While writing for a broad audience, Rethinking Schools emphasizes problems facing urban schools, particularly regarding issues of race. Throughout its history, Rethinking Schools has tried to balance balanced classroom practice and educational theory. It is an activist publication, with articles written by and for teachers, parents, and students. Yet it also addresses key policy issues, such as vouchers and marketplace-oriented reforms, funding equity, and school-to-work (The History and Philosophy, second paragraph).

Brazilian educator Paulo Freire wrote that teachers should attempt to "live part of their dreams within their educational space." Rethinking Schools believes that classrooms can be places of hope, where students and teachers gain glimpses of the kind of society we could live in and learn the academic and critical skills needed to make that vision a reality (The History and Philosophy, fourth paragraph, http://www.rethinkingschools .org/about/history.shtml).

Rethinking Schools also offers many reasonably-priced, teacher-friendly publications including *Rethinking Early Childhood Education, Unlearning "Indian" Stereotypes, A People's History for the Classroom, Rethinking Our Classrooms, Teaching for Equity and Justice— Volume 1 & 2, The Line Between Us: Teaching About the Border and Mexican Immigration, Whose Wars? Teaching about the Iraq War and the War on Terrorism, Rethinking Mathematics, "Special Edition: Kids' Stuff: Preschool and Early Elementary Teachers Connect with Students and Teach for Justice, Rethinking Globalization: Teaching for Justice in an Unjust World,* and *Rethinking Columbus* (www.rethinkingschools.org/publication/ index.shtml).

Teaching for Tolerance
www.tolerance.org
Founded in 1991 by the Southern Poverty Law Center, Teaching Tolerance is dedicated to reducing prejudice, improving intergroup relations, and supporting equitable school experiences for our nation's children. They provide free educational materials to teachers and other school practitioners in the U.S. and abroad. [Their] teaching materials have won two Oscars, an Emmy, and more than 20 honors from the Association of Educational Publishers, including two Golden Lamp Awards, the industry's highest honor. Scientific surveys demonstrate that their programs help students learn respect for differences and bolster teacher practice (http://www .tolerance.org/about).

Its award-winning magazine is distributed free twice a year to more than 400,000 educators, and its innovative multimedia kits are provided at no charge to thousands of schools and community groups (fifth paragraph, http://www .splcenter.org/center/about.jsp).

Topics and DVDs include early grades products, *Rhinos and Raspberries and I Will Be Your Friend*: middle and upper grades products, *Viva La Causa, Mighty Times: The Legacy of Rosa Parks*, and *Mighty Times: The Children's March, One Survivor Remembers*.

Social Justice Math

www.radicalmath.org

Radical Math Teachers are educators who work to integrate issues of economic and social justice into our math classes and we seek to inspire and support other educators to do the same (About RadicalMath, second paragraph). We believe that math literacy is a civil right, and that our nation's failure to provide students, especially low-income youth of color, with a high-quality math education, is a terrible injustice (about RadicalMath, third paragraph). We are committed to making sure our classrooms are nurturing places for all students, that celebrating different cultures, histories, and styles of learning, and that reflect reflecting the just societies we they are hoping to bring about through their own lives and teaching practices (About RadicalMath, fourth paragraph). We encourage our students and teachers to ask the question: "What are the problems that my community is facing and how can I use math to understand and help solve them?" (About RadicalMath, fifth paragraph, http://www.radicalmath.org/main.php?id=about).

On their website you can access and download over seven-hundred lesson plans, articles, charts, graphs, data sets, maps, books, and websites to integrate issues of social and economic justice into math classes and curriculum. You can browse the resources by math topic, social justice issue or resource types.

EdChange

www.EdChange.org

EdChange is team of passionate, experienced, established educators dedicated to equity, diversity, multiculturalism, and social justice. With this shared vision, we have joined to collaborate in order to develop resources, workshops, and projects that contribute to progressive change in ourselves, our schools, and our society (Who We Are, first paragraph, http://www.edchange.org/who.html). We act to shape schools, and communities in which all people, regardless of race, gender, sexual orientation, class, (dis)ability, language, or religion, have equitable opportunities to achieve their fullest and to be safe, valued, affirmed, and empowered (Our Philosophy, first paragraph, http://www.edchange.org/philosophy.html).

The website offers a variety of projects and resources, workshops and consulting services, posters, free handouts, white papers, an e-newsletter, and links to Multicultural Pavilion, SoJust.net (historic speeches, song lyrics, poetry, essays, and other documentary artifacts related to social justice), Social Justice Store, Multicultural Poster Store, and Social Justice Bookstore.

Human Rights Resource Center
www.hrusa.org
The Human Rights Resource Center is an integral part of the University of Minnesota Human Rights Center and works in partnership with the University of Minnesota Human Rights Library to create and distribute Human Rights Education (HRE) resources via electronic and print media (About the Human Rights Resource Center, first paragraph and first bullet). The Human Rights Resource Center makes excellent HRE resources produced by non-profit organizations and independent publishers accessible to all. These resources include more than fifty curricula, guides, videos, documents, and other educational aids (About the Human Rights Resource Center: HR Education Materials).

The Human Rights Education Series provides resources for the ever-growing body of educators and activists seeking to build a culture of human rights in the U.S. and abroad (Human Rights Resource Center: Material Resources: The Human Rights Education Series). The Community Guide offers key discussion activities for Human Rights Commissioners, community leaders, and other interested individuals to better understand these disparities and their causes, as well as to work to overcome them (Human Rights Resource Center: Material Resources: The Community Guide).

The 5-part *Close the Gap* documentary series on race, class, and place disparities is available with companion resources for engaging youth in grades eight-twelve in ways to recognize and eliminate these race, class, and place disparities in our schools and communities. (Human Rights Resource Center: Material Resources: The 5-part Close the Gap . . .)

Public Broadcasting System (PBS)
www.pbs.org/teachers

Public Television's primary mission is to inform and inspire the American public with multi-platform content of unparalleled educational quality. PBS is dedicated to providing you, your students and their families with resources that transform teaching and learning. (About Us, second paragraph) PBS Teachers is PBS' national web destination for high-quality preK-12 educational resources. Here you'll find classroom materials suitable for a wide range of subjects and grade levels. We provide thousands of lesson plans, teaching activities, on-demand video assets, and interactive games and simulations. These resources are correlated to state and national educational standards (About Us: About PBS Teachers: Free Resources for Teaching & Learning second sentence, http://www.pbs.org/teachers/about/).

A general search including all grade levels and resource types, displays results in a significant number of categories: environment (561), race (520), class (325), freedom (326), civil rights (467), poverty (115), immigration (113), gender (88), and globalization (391). I have used several of the interactive activities and video clips.

Constitutional Rights Foundation
www.crf-usa.org

Constitutional Rights Foundation (CRF) seeks to instill in our nation's youth a deeper understanding of citizenship through values expressed in our Constitution and its Bill of Rights and to educate young people to become active and responsible participants in our society (About Constitutional Rights Foundation, first paragraph, http://www.crf-usa.org/about-crf.html).

CRF, a non-profit, non-partisan, community-based organization dedicated to educating America's young people about the importance of civic participation in a democratic society (About Constitutional Rights Foundation, second paragraph). CRF's publications and materials provide classroom teachers and students with high-quality content and thought-provoking questioning strategies to promote critical-thinking development, open discussion of issues, and interactive activities to heighten learning. When addressing controversial contemporary or historical issues, we strive to provide a balanced presentation and multiple perspectives. Most of our lessons

Teachers can search and download hundreds of lessons on a variety of topics: Bill of Rights in Action, School Violence, Terrorism, Iraq, Brown v. Board, Immigration, Election, Constitution, Impeachment, and Service Learning. I reviewed the forty-five page unit *Current Issues in Immigration* 2008 and found it informative and well-balanced, presenting the critical issues and perspectives and engaging students in critical thinking through discussion and role playing. Teachers can also subscribe to a free quarterly newsletter Bill of Rights in Action. The website has links to this month in history, quotes of the month, and ideas for using quotes in the classroom.

directly address national and state standards (Publications: Free Lessons also Free Lessons Index, http://www.crf-usa.org/publications/).

Office of Social Justice, Catholic Charities
www.osjspm.org
The mission of the Archdiocese of St. Paul and Minneapolis' Office of Social Justice is to aid those most in need through a call to justice.

This website has a variety of tools and resources for schools, churches, and social justice committees, including understanding poverty, charity and justice, reflection and action, and a toolkit for young advocates, including a six-lesson curriculum on poverty and steps they can take to work with the poor in eliminating the causes of poverty.

They also have compiled fact sheets with basic information on a variety of social issues to provide data for problem analysis, reflection, and action. Topics include child care, federal budget, foreign aid, global warming, health care, housing, immigration, low wage workers, minimum wage survey, Minnesota minimum wage FAQ and survey, taxes, and welfare. The site provides links and resources for broader issues such as landmines, sweatshops, predatory lending, labor rights, citizenship, criminal justice, death penalty, and socially responsible investing.

Minneapolis Foundation
www.mplsfoundation.org
The Minneapolis Foundation is a community foundation that invests and distributes charitable funds created by members of the community (About Us, third paragraph, http://www.minneapolisfoundation.org/AboutUs/Mission.html). It also has a history of helping citizens explore tough issues from new perspectives and participate in collective efforts for charity and

social justice, recognizing in one another a common spirit and responsibility. (Community Issues, first paragraph, http://www.minneapolisfoundation.org/Community/Overview.html).

Through the "community issues" link, educators can find information such as fact sheets on housing and homelessness, education, racial and economic equity, immigration, and youth violence.

The Advocates for Human Rights
www.theadvocatesforhumanrights.org
Minnesota Advocates for Human Rights
www.mnadvocates.org
and *Discover Human Rights™ Institute*
www.discoverhumanrights.org
The Advocates for Human Rights is a non-profit organization dedicated to promoting and protecting human rights. Through cutting-edge research, education, and advocacy The Advocates saves lives, fights injustice, restores peace, and builds the human rights movement in the United States and around the world. The Advocates for Human Rights established the Discover Human Rights™ Institute in 2007. The Institute provides educational resources and tools to help people learn about and apply international human rights standards in their daily lives, families, workplaces, and communities. (About the Discover Human Rights Institute, first paragraph, http://www.discoverhumanrights.org/About.html). With resource links organized by topic for educators, students, and advocates, this site offers lesson plans, fact sheets, quizzes, ideas for action, a free newsletter, and a Discover Human Rights toolkit.

Youth for Human Rights
www.youthforhumanrights.org
Youth for Human Rights International teaches human rights education both in the classroom and beyond traditional education settings. We aim to reach people from diverse backgrounds and our materials often appeal across generations. From teaching human rights through conferences and workshops to hip-hop and dancing, the message spreads around the world and reaches onto every continent and into many countries (http://www.youthforhumanrights.org/about/index.html). Educators may download or request a DVD of thirty public service announcements, and an information package in one of thirteen different languages.

Michigan Department of Education
www.michigan.gov/mde

The Michigan Department of Education defines core democratic values for elementary, middle school, and older students including common good, justice, liberty, life, equality, diversity, pursuit of happiness, popular sovereignty, truth, patriotism, and rule of law. It also describes the fundamental beliefs and principles of a constitutional democracy (Core_democtaric_Values_48832_7.pdf).

Service-Learning Organizations and Resources

National Youth Leadership Council (NYLC)
www.nylc.org

For more than 25 years, NYLC has led a movement that links youth, educators, and communities to redefine the roles of young people in society. That movement is service-learning, and it empowers youth to transform themselves from recipients of information and resources into valuable, contributing members of a democracy.

Each year, thousands of service-learning practitioners improve their practice with the help of NYLC. The National Service-Learning Conference draws nearly 3,000 attendees from around the world for three intensive days of speakers, workshops, and networking. Growing to Greatness publishes research that is transforming the field of service-learning and influencing public policy. And the Generator School Network is reshaping the way teachers and students conduct service-learning (http://www.nylc.org/pages-aboutus).

Campus Compact
www.compact.org

Campus Compact is a national coalition of more than 1,100 college and university presidents—representing some 6 million students—who are committed to fulfilling the civic purposes of higher education. Campus Compact advances the public purposes of colleges and universities by deepening their ability to improve community life and to educate students for civic and social responsibility (Who We Are: Mission, http://www.compact.org/about/history-mission-vision/).

Michigan Journal of Community Service Learning (MJCSL)
www.umich.edu/~mjcsl

The MJCSL is a national, peer-reviewed journal for college and university faculty and administrators, with an editorial board of faculty from many academic disciplines and professional fields at the University of Michigan and other U.S. higher education institutions.

Since 1994, the Michigan Journal has endeavored to publish the highest quality research, theory, and pedagogy articles related to higher education academic service-learning (About the MJCSL, http://www.umich.edu/~mjcsl/about.html).

Corporation of National and Community Service
www.nationalservice.gov and www.serve.gov

In 1993, the Corporation for National and Community Service was established. The Corporation was created to connect Americans of all ages and backgrounds with opportunities to give back to their communities and their nation. It merged the work and staffs of two predecessor agencies, ACTION and the Commission on National and Community Service (Our History and Legislation, http://www.nationalservice.gov/about/role_impact/history.asp). The mission of the Corporation for National and Community Service is to improve lives, strengthen communities, and foster civic engagement through service and volunteering (About Us and Our Programs: Our Mission and Guiding Principles, http://www.nationalservice.gov/about/role_impact/mission.asp).

Learn and Serve America's National Service-Learning Clearinghouse (NSLC)
www.servicelearning.org
America's Most Comprehensive Service-Learning Resource

Learn and Serve America's National Service-Learning Clearinghouse (NSLC) supports the service-learning community in higher education, kindergarten through grade twelve, community-based initiatives and tribal programs, as well as all others interested in strengthening schools and communities using service-learning techniques and methodologies.

The Clearinghouse maintains a website with timely information and relevant resources to support service-learning programs, practitioners, and researchers. The Clearinghouse operates national email discussion lists for K-12, cbo, tribes and territories, and higher education service-learning to encourage discussion and exchange of ideas. The Clearinghouse also maintains an ever-growing library collection that is available to Learn and Serve America grantees and subgrantees (About NSLC http://www.servicelearning.org/about_us/about_nslc/index.php).

*Sections in text boxes are author's comments. All other text is from the original source, as cited, from listed website sources. Information in parenthesis indicates the section of the Web site from which the information was obtained.

APPENDIX B

Suggested Readings

Service-Learning and Civic Engagement

Dewey, John. *Democracy and Education*. New York: The Free Press, 1916.

Kahne, Joseph, and Joel Westheimer. "In Service of What? The Politics of Service Learning." *Phi Delta Kappan* 77 (1996): 592–98. http://vnweb.hwwilsonweb.com .ezproxy.stthomas.edu/hww/results/getResults.jhtml?_DARGS=/hww/results/ results_common.jhtml.33 (accessed November 22, 2009).

Kaye, Cathryn Berger. *The Complete Guide to Service Learning: Proven, Practical Ways to Engage Students in Civic Responsibility, Academic Curriculum, and Social Action.* Minneapolis: Free Spirit, 2004.

Lewis, Barbara A. *The Kid's Guide to Social Action: How to Solve the Social Problems You Choose—And Turn Creative Thinking into Positive Action.* Minneapolis: Free Spirit, 1998.

O'Grady, Carolyn, ed. *Integrating Service Learning and Multicultural Education in Colleges and Universities.* Mahwah, N.J.: Erlbaum, 2000.

Education, Diversity, and Multicultural Education

Adams, Maurianne, Lee Anne Bell, and Pat Griffin, eds. *Teaching for Diversity and Social Justice: A Sourcebook.* New York: Routledge, 1997.

Adams, Maurianne, Warren J. Blumenfeld, Rosie Castañeda, Heather W. Hackman, Madeline L. Peters, and Ximena Zuniga, eds. *Readings for Diversity and Social Justice: An Anthology on Racism, Antisemitism, Sexism, Heterosexism, Ableism, and Classism.* New York: Routledge, 2000.

Connell, R. W. *Masculinities.* Berkeley: University of California Press, 1995.

hooks, bell. *Feminist Theory: From Margin to the Center*. Cambridge, Mass.: South End Press, 2000.

hooks, bell. *Where We Stand: Class Matters*. New York: Routledge, 2000.

Kivel Paul. *Uprooting Racism: How White People Can Work for Racial Justice*. Gabriola Island, BC: New Society, 1996.

Lee, Enid, Deborah Menkart, and Margo Okazawa-Rey, eds. *Beyond Heroes and Holidays: A Practical Guide to K–12 Anti-Racist, Multicultural Education and Staff Development*. Washington, D.C.: Network of Educators of the Americas, 1998.

Loewen, James W. *Lies My Teacher Told Me: Everything Your American History Teacher Got Wrong*. New York: Simon and Schuster, 1995.

McIntosh, Peggy. "White Privilege: Unpacking the Invisible Knapsack." In *White Privilege: Essential Readings on the Other Side of Racism*, edited by Paula Rothenberg, 109–13. New York: Worth, 1988.

Pollock, Mica, ed. *Everyday Antiracism: Getting Real about Race in School*. New York: New Press, 2008.

Rothenberg, Paula, ed. *White Privilege: Essential Readings on the Other Side of Racism*. New York: Worth, 2005.

Schniedewind, Nancy, and Ellen Davidson. *Open Minds to Equality: A Sourcebook of Learning Activities to Affirm Diversity and Promote Equity*. 3rd ed. Milwaukee: Rethinking Schools, 2006.

Sleeter, Christine E., and Carl A. Grant. *Making Choices for Multicultural Education: Five Approaches to Race, Class and Gender*. Hoboken, N.J.: Wiley, 2009.

Takaki, Ronald. *A Different Mirror: A History of Multicultural America*. Boston: Little, Brown, 1993.

West, Cornel. *Race Matters*. 1993. Reprint, New York: Vintage Books, 2001.

Wise, Tim. *Speaking Treason Fluently: Anti-Racist Reflections from an Angry White Male*. Berkeley, Calif.: Soft Skull Press, 2008.

Zinn, Howard. *A People's History of the United States, 1492–Present*. New York: HarperCollins, 1999.

Critical Education and Critical Social Theory

Apple, Michael W. *Ideology and Curriculum*. 1979. New York: Routledge, 1990.

Bourdieu, Pierre, and Jean Claude Passeron. *Reproduction in Education, Society and Culture*. 1977. London: Sage, 2000.

Darder, Antonia, Marta Baltodano, and Rodolfo D. Torres, eds. *The Critical Pedagogy Reader*. New York: Routledge Falmer, 2003.

Foucault, Michel. *Discipline and Punish: The Birth of the Prison*. Translated by A. Sheridan. New York: Random House, 1975.

Freire, Paulo. *Pedagogy of Freedom: Ethics, Democracy and Civic Courage*. Translated by P. Clarke. Lanham, Md.: Rowman and Littlefield, 1998.

Gramsci, Antonio. *The Antonio Gramsci Reader*, edited by D. Forgacs. New York: New York University Press, 2000.

Luke, Carmen, and Jennifer Gore, eds. *Feminisms and Critical Pedagogy*. New York: Routledge, 1992.

Macedo, Donaldo, and Lilia I. Bartholome. *Dancing with Bigotry: Beyond the Politics of Tolerance*. New York: St. Martin's, 1999.

Mayo, Peter. *Gramsci, Freire, and Adult Education: Possibilities for Transformative Action*. New York: Zed Books, 1999.

Shor, Ira. *When Students Have Power*. Chicago: University of Chicago Press, 1996.

Seven Principles of Catholic Social Teachings

The Church's social teaching is a rich treasure of wisdom about building a just society and living lives of holiness amidst the challenges of modern society. Modern Catholic social teaching has been articulated through a tradition of papal, conciliar, and episcopal documents. The depth and richness of this tradition can be understood best through a direct reading of these documents. These brief reflections highlight several of the key themes that are at the heart of our Catholic social tradition.

1. Life and Dignity of the Human Person

The Catholic Church proclaims that human life is sacred and that the dignity of the human person is the foundation of a moral vision for society. Our belief in the sanctity of human life and the inherent dignity of the human person is the foundation of all the principles of our social teaching. In our society, human life is under direct attack from abortion and assisted suicide. The value of human life is being threatened by increasing use of the death penalty. We believe that every person is precious, that people are more important than things, and that the measure of every institution is whether it threatens or enhances the life and dignity of the human person.

2. Call to Family, Community, and Participation

The person is not only sacred but also social. How we organize our society in economics and politics, in law and policy directly affects human dignity and the capacity of individuals to grow in community. The family is the central social institution that must be supported and strengthened, not undermined. We believe people have a right and a duty to participate in society, seeking together the common good and well-being of all, especially the poor and vulnerable.

3. Rights and Responsibilities

The Catholic tradition teaches that human dignity can be protected and a healthy community can be achieved only if human rights are protected and responsibilities are met. Therefore, every person has a fundamental right to life and a right to those things required for human decency. Corresponding to these rights are duties and responsibilities to one another, to our families, and to the larger society.

4. Option for the Poor and Vulnerable

A basic moral test is how our most vulnerable members are faring. In a society marred by deepening divisions between rich and poor, our tradition recalls the story of the Last Judgment (Mt 25:31–46) and instructs us to put the needs of the poor and vulnerable first.

5. The Dignity of Work and the Rights of Workers

The economy must serve people, not the other way around. Work is more than a way to make a living; it is a form of continuing participation in God's creation. If the dignity of work is to be protected, then the basic rights of workers must be respected[:] the right to productive work, to decent and fair wages, to organize and join unions, to private property, and to economic initiative.

6. Solidarity

We are our brothers' and sisters' keepers, wherever they live. We are one human family, whatever our national, racial, ethnic, economic, and ideological differences. Learning to practice the virtue of solidarity means learning that "loving our neighbor" has global dimensions in an interdependent world.

7. Care for God's Creation

We show our respect for the Creator by our stewardship of creation. Care for the earth is not just an Earth Day slogan, it is a requirement of our faith. We are called to protect people and the planet, living our faith in relationship with all of God's creation. This environmental challenge has fundamental moral and ethical dimensions that cannot be ignored.

At archdiocesesantafe.org/Offices/SocialJustice/SocialTeaching.html (accessed July 20, 2009).

Glossary

activism: An action to affect change that brings about social, economic, political, or environmental justice. The action may be internal—changing one's own actions—or external—working to change a policy or system. Activists may take public actions, such as letter campaigns, lobbying, protests, or awareness campaigns, or they may work on an individual basis to change others' opinions and behaviors.

agency: The belief that you can affect change and the knowledge that what you do makes a difference.

allies: Individuals who seek to educate themselves and others in dominant groups about their power and privilege in relation to injustice and oppression, and who support those in subordinate groups in their struggles.

altruism: Helping others without any expectation of personal benefit.

caring: Becoming personally and emotionally invested in others' welfare and making oneself available to those who need help in the context of a mutual relationship.

Catholic social teachings: A set of seven principles based on Scripture and Church documents that serve as a guide for building a just society. (See the notes for chapter 8 for specific delineation of these principles.)

charity: Extending generosity or kindness to those who are in need or suffering.

community service: Volunteering in the community, which is distinguished from service-learning because the emphasis is providing a service, without the academic connection.

compassion: The "capacity to connect with and be moved by another's pain . . . which moves one to action."[1]

counterhegemony: Revolutionary beliefs and actions, which make the invisible visible, leading to social and political change. In society and education, counterhegemonic practices challenge the dominant culture and provide sites at the grassroots level for individuals and groups to resist and change the system.

critical: Stephen D. Brookfield insists, whether in critical learning, critical analysis, or critical reflection, that for it to be "critical" individuals must examine power relations inherent in the situation or context, question the underlying assumptions on race, gender, and class, and understand its connection to the dominant ideology.[2]

critical consciousness: Developing a more accurate understanding of the world. The four elements of critical-consciousness development are developing a deeper awareness of self, developing a deeper awareness and broader perspective of others, developing a deeper awareness and broader perspective of social issues, and seeing one's potential to make change.

critical multiculturalism: The goal of critical multiculturalism is to become aware of the social, economic, and political forces that have shaped society in order to challenge the policies and practices that create and reproduce inequity and injustice.

critical pedagogy: A democratic approach to education that empowers students as codevelopers and active participants in the learning process. Teachers guide students in a process of critical inquiry, reflection, and action in order to create a society based on freedom, equality, and justice.

critical social theory: Promotes a critique of schooling, social institutions, and cultural norms, proposing a liberatory education that illuminates the role of power in maintaining the status quo of dominant and oppressed groups of people. Critical theorists assess the social construction of knowledge and truth in the curriculum and examine how power and control is exercised to produce a "common sense" acceptance of what is normal and legitimate.

Additionally, critical social theorists expose how ideologies that reproduce social structures are transmitted, and they encourage teachers to promote democratic values by articulating the purpose of education, problematizing reality, linking learning experience to the larger community, and empowering students with critical-thinking skills and opportunities to engage in activities for radical democracy.

efficacy: Belief in one's capacity to succeed.

empathy: "The ability to understand and share another's feelings."[3]

hegemony: Social norms, cultural messages, and "common sense" explanations that represent the interests of a dominant group and serve to reproduce the status quo based on subordination and inequality of others. Because the hegemonic messages are so ingrained in society and supported by schools, churches, media, and other social and political structures, they prevent us from seeing the role power and privilege play in oppressive relations. A few examples include the following: "this is a free society"; "the poor are to blame for their situation"; and "women just aren't as good leaders as men."

meritocracy: The belief that individuals are rewarded according to their talent and work rather than on their family background. This ideology claims that all have an equal chance at the American dream: if they are persistent and work hard, they will succeed. Meritocracy is exposed as a myth by examining the rates of wealth, education, poverty, and homelessness by socioeconomic, racial, gender, and ethnic backgrounds.

multicultural education: Multicultural education broadens curriculum to include multiple perspectives, places the student at the center of the learning process, and advances policies that create an inclusive, equitable environment where all students are valued and can achieve academic success. Multicultural education requires examining one's beliefs, one's attitudes, and the biases and assumptions that permeate society, in order to promote justice and end discrimination.

praxis: Critical reflection and action with the goal of social change for equity and justice. "Critical educators argue that *praxis* (informed actions) must be guided by *phronesis* (the disposition to act truly and rightly) . . . [meaning] actions and knowledge must be directed at eliminating pain, oppression, and inequality, and at promoting justice and freedom."[4]

service-learning: A learning strategy in which students have leadership roles in thoughtfully organized service experiences that meet real needs in the community. The service is integrated into the students' academic studies with structured time to research, reflect, discuss, and connect their experiences to their learning and their worldview. Service-learning, also called *community-based learning*, is often confused with community service and volunteerism. The major difference is the intentional connection to student learning, with information, preparation, and reflection before, during, and after.

social justice: "Promoting social justice means contributing to social change and public policies that will increase gender and racial equality, end discrimination of various kinds, and reduce the stark income inequalities that characterize this country and most of the world."[5]

Notes

Preface

1. Council for Secular Humanism, "The Affirmations of Humanism: A Statement of Principles," at www.secularhumanism.org/index.php?section=main&page=affirma tions (accessed September 21, 2009).

2. Alexander W. Astin, Linda J. Sax, and Juan Avalos, "Long-Term Effects of Volunteerism during the Undergraduate Years," *The Review of Higher Education* 22 (1999): 187–202; Shelley H. Billig, "Research on K–12 School-Based Service-Learning: The Evidence Builds," *Phi Delta Kappan* 81 (2000): 658–64, http://fc9en6ys2q.search.serial ssolutions.com.ezproxy.stthomas.edu/?sid=CentralSearch:EAP&genre=article&atitle= Research+on+K-12+School-Based+Service-Learning.&volume=81&issue=9&title= Phi+Delta+Kappan&issn=0031-7217&date=2000-05-01&spage=658&aulast=Billig &aufirst=Shelley (accessed November 25, 2009); and Janet Eyler and Dwight E. Giles, Jr., *Where's the Learning in Service-Learning?* (San Francisco: Jossey-Bass, 1999).

3. Marilynne Boyle-Baise, *Multicultural Service Learning: Educating Teachers in Diverse Communities* (New York: Teachers College Press, 2002); and Miranda Yates and James Youniss., eds., *Roots of Civic Identity: International Perspectives on Community Service and Activism in Youth* (Cambridge: Cambridge University Press, 2003).

4. Carolyn O'Grady, "Integrating Service Learning and Multicultural Education: An Overview," in *Integrating Service Learning and Multicultural Education in Colleges and Universities*, ed. Carolyn O'Grady (Mahwah, N.J.: Erlbaum, 2000), 1–19; Karen Warren, "Educating Students for Social Justice in Service Learning," *Journal of Experiential Education* 21, no. 3 (1998): 134–39; and Wokie Weah, Verna Cornelia Simmons, and McClellan Hall, "Service-Learning and Multicultural/Multiethnic Perspectives: From Diversity to Equity," *Phi Delta Kappan* 81, no. 9 (2000): 673–75.

5. Marilynne Boyle-Baise and Christine E. Sleeter, "Community-Based Service Learning for Multicultural Teacher Education," *Educational Foundation* 14, no. 2 (2000): 33–50.

6. Marilynne Boyle-Baise, "Community Service-Learning for Multicultural Education: An Exploratory Study with Preservice Teachers," *Equity and Excellence* 32 (1998): 52–60.

7. Marilynne Boyle-Baise and James Langford, "There Are Children Here: Service-Learning for Social Justice," *Equity and Excellence* 37, no. 1 (2004): 55–66.

8. Boyle-Baise, *Multicultural Service Learning*; Joseph Kahne and Joel Westheimer, "In Service of What? The Politics of Service Learning," *Phi Delta Kappan 77* (1996): 592–98, http://vnweb.hwwilsonweb.com.ezproxy.stthomas.edu/hww/results/get Results.jhtml?_DARGS=/hww/results/results_common.jhtml.33 (accessed November 22, 2009).; Joseph Kahne, Joel Westheimer, and Bethany Rogers, "Service-Learning and Citizenship: Directions for Research," special issue, *Michigan Journal of Community Service Learning* 7 (2000): 42–51; and Edward Metz, Jeffrey McLellan, and James Youniss, "Types of Voluntary Service and Adolescents' Civic Development," *Journal of Adolescent Research* 18 (2003): 188–203.

9. Herbert L. Martin and Terri A. Wheeler, "Social Justice, Service-Learning, and Multiculturalism as Inseparable Companions," in *Integrating Service Learning and Multicultural Education in Colleges and Universities*, ed. Carolyn O'Grady (Mahwah, N.J.: Erlbaum, 2000), 135–52; Carol Wiechman Maybach, "Investigating Urban Community Needs: Service Learning from a Social Justice Perspective," *Education and Urban Society* 28 (1996): 224–36; and Cynthia Rosenberger, "Beyond Empathy: Developing Critical Consciousness through Service Learning," in *Integrating Service Learning and Multicultural Education in Colleges and Universities*, ed. Carolyn O'Grady (Mahwah, N.J.: Erlbaum, 2000), 135–52.

10. Eyler and Giles, *Where's the Learning in Service-learning?*; Kahne, Westheimer, and Rogers, "Service-Learning and Citizenship"; Metz, McLellan, and Youniss, "Types of Voluntary Service and Adolescents' Civic Development"; Kim Patrick Moore and Judith Haymore Sandholtz, "Designing Successful Service Learning Projects for Urban Schools," *Urban Education* 34, no. 4 (1999): 480–98; and Lori J. Vogelgesang and Alexander W. Astin, "Comparing the Effects of Community Service and Service Learning," *Michigan Journal of Community Service Learning* 7, no. 1 (2000): 25–34.

11. Complete information on the study, *Service-Learning and Social Justice: Effects of Early Experience*, can be found in PDF format on the ProQuest Dissertation and Theses Database, http://vnweb.hwwilsonweb.com.ezproxy.stthomas.edu/hww/results/ getResults.jhtml?_DARGS=/hww/results/results_common.jhtml.33.

Chapter 1

1. Stephen D. Brookfield, "Transformative Learning as Ideological Critique," in *Learning as Transformation: Critical Perspectives on a Theory in Progress*, ed. Jack Mezirow (San Francisco: Jossey-Bass, 2000), 125–48; and Stephen D. Brookfield,

The Power of Critical Theory: Liberating Adult Learning and Teaching (San Francisco: Jossey-Bass, 2005).

2. Susan Cipolle, "Service-Learning as a Counter-Hegemonic Practice: Evidence Pro and Con," *Multicultural Education* 11, no. 3 (2004): 12–23.

3. National Youth Leadership Council, "What Is Service Learning?" at nylc .org/wisl/index.html (accessed August 17, 2009).

4. James A. Banks and Cherry A. McGee Banks, eds., *Multicultural Education: Issues and Perspectives*, 3rd ed. (Hoboken, N.J.: Wiley, 1997).

5. Sonia Nieto, *Affirming Diversity: The Sociopolitical Context of Multicultural Education* (New York: Addison Wesley Longman, 2000).

6. Joe Kincheloe and Shirley R. Steinberg, *Changing Multiculturalism: New Times, New Curriculum* (Bristol, Pa.: Open University Press, 1997).

7. Carl A. Grant and Christine E. Sleeter, "Race, Class, Gender and Disability in the Classroom," in *Multicultural Education: Issues and Perspectives*, ed. James A. Banks and Cherry A. McGee Banks, 3rd ed. (Hoboken, N.J.: Wiley, 1997): 61–80.

8. bell hooks and Cornel West, *Breaking Bread: Insurgent Black Intellectual Life* (Toronto: Between the Lines, 1991).

9. Robert A. Rhoads, "Critical Multiculturalism and Service Learning," in *Academic Service Learning: A Pedagogy of Action and Reflections*, ed. Robert A. Rhoads and Jeffrey P.F. Howard (San Francisco: Jossey-Bass, 1998): 39–45.

10. Leda Cooks, Erica Scharrer, and Mari Castaneda Paredes, "Toward a Social Approach to Learning in Community Service Learning," *Michigan Journal of Community Service Learning* 10, no. 2 (2004): 44–56.

11. Cipolle, "Service-Learning as a Counter-Hegemonic Practice."

12. Susan Cipolle, "Service-Learning and Social Justice: Effects of Early Experiences" (PhD diss., University of St. Thomas, 2006).

13. Anne Colby and others, eds., *Educating Citizens: Preparing America's Undergraduates for Lives of Moral and Civic Responsibility* (San Francisco: Jossey-Bass, 2003).

14. Peter McLaren, *Life in Schools: An Introduction to Critical Pedagogy in the Foundations of Education* (New York: Longman, 1998).

15. Giroux, H. A., *Teachers as Intellectuals: Toward a Critical Pedagogy of Learning* (Westport, Conn.: Bergin and Garvey, 1988).

16. Online Etymology Dictionary, at www.etymonline.com (accessed August 21, 2009).

17. Bernard Bailyn, *Education in the Forming of American Society* (New York: Vintage Books, 1960), cited in Thomas Groome, *Educating for Life: A Spiritual Vision for Every Teacher and Parent* (New York: Crossroad Publishing, 1998).

18. Following the lead of Sonia Nieto in *Affirming Diversity* and Beverly Tatum in *Why Are All the Black Kids Sitting Together in the Cafeteria?* I have chosen to capitalize the terms *White* and *Black* in the context of this book because the terms refer to groups of people. I want to affirm the importance and interconnections of one's cultural, ethnic, and racial identities; but in a racialized society, it is necessary to

recognize that even though race does not exist biologically, skin color is a relevant factor in life experiences.

19. For information on civic, political-moral identity formation through community service in a predominantly Black, middle class Catholic high-school population, I refer you to the work of Miranda Yates and James Younnis. Yates and Youniss, "Community Service and Political-Moral Identity in Adolescents," *Journal of Research on Adolescence* 6 (1996): 271–84; Yates and Youniss, "A Developmental Perspective on Community Service in Youth," *Social Development* 5 (1996): 85–111; and Yates, "Community Service and Political-Moral Discussions Among Adolescents: A Study of a Mandatory School-Based Program in the United States," in *Roots of Civic Identity: International Perspectives on Community Service and Activism in Youth*, ed. Yates and Youniss (Cambridge: Cambridge University Press, 2003): 16–31.

Chapter 2

1. Research findings from Susan Cipolle, "Service-Learning and Social Justice: Effects of Early Experiences" (PhD diss., University of St. Thomas, 2006).

Chapter 3

1. Daphna Oyserman and Hazel Markus, "The Sociocultural Self," in *Psychological Perspectives on the Self*, vol. 4, *The Self in Social Perspective*, ed. Jerry Suls (Hillsdale, N.J.: Erlbaum, 1993): 187–219.

2. Oyserman and Markus, "The Sociocultural Self"; and Robert A. Rhoads, *Community Service and Higher Learning: Explorations of the Caring Self* (Albany: State University of New York Press, 1997).

3. Erik H. Erikson, *Identity: Youth and Crisis* (New York: Norton, 1968).

4. Sharon Daloz Parks, *Big Questions, Worthy Dreams: Mentoring Young Adults in Their Search for Meaning, Purpose, and Faith* (San Francisco: Jossey-Bass, 2000).

5. Laurent A. Daloz and others, *Common Fire: Leading Lives of Commitment in a Complex World* (Boston: Beacon Press, 1996).

6. Timothy K. Stanton, Dwight E. Giles, and Nadinne I. Cruz, *Service-Learning: A Movement's Pioneers Reflect on Its Origins, Practice, and Future* (San Francisco: Jossey-Bass, 1999).

7. Laurent A. Daloz, "Transformative Learning for the Common Good," in *Learning as Transformation: Critical Perspectives on a Theory in Progress*, ed. Jack Mezirow (San Francisco: Jossey-Bass, 2000); and Oyserman and Markus, "The Sociocultural Self."

8. Markus, H., and Nurius, P., "Possible Selves," *American Psychologist*, cited in Anne Colby and others, eds., *Educating Citizens: Preparing America's Undergraduates for Lives of Moral and Civic Responsibility* (San Francisco: Jossey-Bass, 2003).

9. Miranda Yates and James Youniss, eds., *Roots of Civic Identity: International Perspectives on Community Service and Activism in Youth* (Cambridge: Cambridge University Press, 2003).

10. Yates and Youniss, *Roots of Civic Identity*.

11. Verba, Schlozman, and Brady, cited in Miranda Yates and James Youniss, eds., *Roots of Civic Identity: International Perspectives on Community Service and Activism in Youth* (Cambridge: Cambridge University Press, 2003).

12. Yates and Youniss, *Roots of Civic Identity*.

13. Anne Colby and others, eds., *Educating Citizens: Preparing America's Undergraduates for Lives of Moral and Civic Responsibility* (San Francisco: Jossey-Bass, 2003).

14. Colby and others, *Educating Citizens*.

15. Yates & Youniss, cited in Anne Colby and others, eds., *Educating Citizens: Preparing America's Undergraduates for Lives of Moral and Civic Responsibility* (San Francisco: Jossey-Bass, 2003).

16. Parks, *Big Questions, Worthy Dreams*.

17. Parks, *Big Questions, Worthy Dreams*.

18. Colby and others, *Educating Citizens*.

19. Colby and others, *Educating Citizens*.

Chapter 4

1. Samuel P. Oliner and Peral M. Oliner, *The Altruistic Personality: Rescuers of Jews in Nazi Europe* (New York: Free Press, 1990) cited in Daloz, *Common Fire*.

2. Felix Warneken and Michael Tomasello, "Altruistic Helping in Human Infants and Young Chimpanzees," *Science* 311, no. 5765 (3 March 2006): 1301–3.

3. Joseph Kahne and Joel Westheimer, "In Service of What? The Politics of Service Learning," *Phi Delta Kappan* 77 (1996): 592–98, http://vnweb.hwwilsonweb .com.ezproxy.stthomas.edu/hww/results/getResults.jhtml?_DARGS=/hww/results/results_common.jhtml.33; and Wokie Weah, Verna Cornelia Simmons, and Mc-Clellan Hall, "Service-Learning and Multicultural/Multiethnic Perspectives: From Diversity to Equity," *Phi Delta Kappan* 81, no. 9 (2000): 673–75.

4. Christopher J. Koliba, "Service-Learning and Downsizing of Democracy: Learning Our Way Out," *Michigan Journal of Community Service Learning* 10, no. 2 (2004): 57–68; Tony Robinson, "Dare the School Build a New Social Order?" *Michigan Journal of Community Service Learning* 7 (Fall 2000): 142–57; Randy Stoeker, "Community-Based Research: From Practice to Theory and Back Again," *Michigan Journal of Community Service Learning* 9, no. 2 (2003): 35–46; Kahne and Westheimer, "In Service of What?"; and in *Service Learning for Youth Empowerment and Social Change*, ed. Jeff Claus and Curtis Ogden (New York: Peter Lang, 1999).

5. Stoeker, "Community-Based Research."

6. Stoeker, "Community-Based Research."

7. Koliba, "Service-Learning and Downsizing of Democracy"; Robinson, "Dare the School Build a New Social Order?"; and Stoeker, "Community-Based Research."

8. Robinson, "Dare the School Build a New Social Order?"; and Verna Cornelia Simmons and Wokie Roberts-Weah, "Service-Learning and Social Reconstructionism: A Critical Opportunity for Leadership," in *Integrating Service Learning and Multicultural Education in Colleges and Universities*, ed. Carolyn O'Grady (Mahwah, N.J.: Erlbaum, 2000), 189–208.

9. Marilynne Boyle-Baise, *Multicultural Service Learning: Educating Teachers in Diverse Communities* (New York: Teachers' College Press, 2002); Paulo Freire, *Pedagogy of the Oppressed*, trans. M. B. Ramos (1970; repr., New York: Continuum, 1993); Paulo Freire, *Education for Critical Consciousness*, trans. M. B. Ramos (1973; repr., New York: Continuum, 2002); Keith Morton and John Saltmarsh, "Addams, Day, and Dewey: The Emergence of Community Service in American Culture," *Michigan Journal of Community Service Learning* 4 (Fall 1997): 137–49; Carolyn O'Grady, "Integrating Service Learning and Multicultural Education: An Overview," in *Integrating Service Learning and Multicultural Education in Colleges and Universities*, ed. Carolyn O'Grady (Mahwah, N.J.: Erlbaum, 2000), 1–19; John Saltmarsh, "Education for Critical Citizenship: John Dewey's Contribution to the Pedagogy of Community Service-Learning," *Michigan Journal of Community Service Learning* 3 (Fall 1996): 13–21; Henry A. Giroux, *Teachers as Intellectuals: Toward a Critical Pedagogy of Learning* (Westport, Conn.: Bergin and Garvey, 1988); bell hooks, *Teaching to Transgress: Education as the Practice of Freedom* (New York: Routledge, 1994); Peter McLaren, *Life in Schools: An Introduction to Critical Pedagogy in the Foundations of Education* (New York: Longman, 1998); Sonia Nieto, *Affirming Diversity: The Sociopolitical Context of Multicultural Education* (New York: Addison Wesley Longman, 2000); Ira Shor, *Empowering Education: Critical Teaching for Social Change* (Chicago: University of Chicago Press, 1992); and Christine E. Sleeter, *Multicultural Education as Social Activism* (Albany: State University of New York Press, 1996).

10. Richard M. Battistani, "The Service Learner as Engaged Citizen," *Metropolitan Universities: An International Forum* 7, no. 1 (Summer 1996): 85–98; Jeff Claus and Curtis Ogden, "An Empowering, Transformative Approach to Service," in *Service Learning for Youth Empowerment and Social Change*, ed. Jeff Claus and Curtis Ogden (New York: Peter Lang, 1999), 69–93; Henry A. Giroux and Peter L. McLaren, "Introduction," in *Critical Pedagogy, the State and Cultural Struggle*, ed. Henry A. Giroux and Peter L. McLaren (Albany: State University of New York Press, 1989), xi–xxxv; and Rahima C. Wade, "Social Action in the Social Studies: From the Ideal to the Real," *Theory into Practice* 40, no. 1 (2001): 23–28.

11. Joseph Kahne, Joel Westheimer, and Bethany Rogers, "Service-Learning and Citizenship: Directions for Research," special issue, *Michigan Journal of Community Service Learning* 7 (2000): 42–51.

12. Marilynne Boyle-Baise, "Community Service-Learning for Multicultural Education: An Exploratory Study with Preservice Teachers," *Equity and Excellence* 32 (1998): 52–60; Christine E. Sleeter, "Strengthening Multicultural Education with

Community-Based Service Learning," in *Integrating Service Learning and Multicultural Education in Colleges and Universities*, ed. Carolyn O'Grady (Mahwah, N.J.: Erlbaum, 2000), 263–76; Wade, "Social Action in the Social Studies"; and Weah, Simmons, and Hall, "Service-Learning and Multicultural/Multiethnic Perspectives."

13. Sonia Nieto, "Foreword," in *Integrating Service Learning and Multicultural Education in Colleges and Universities*, ed. Carolyn O'Grady (Mahwah, N.J.: Erlbaum, 2000), ix–xi.

14. *Cambridge Dictionary of American English*, http://dictionary.cambridge.org/results.asp?searchword=care&x=0&y=0 (accessed November 28, 2009).

15. Nel Noddings, *Caring: A Feminine Approach to Ethics and Moral Education* (Berkeley: University of California Press, 1984).

16. Carol Gilligan, *In a Different Voice: Psychological Theory and Women's Development* (Cambridge, Mass.: Harvard University Press, 1982).

17. Robert J. Cipolle, Linda M. Strand, and Peter C. Morley, *Pharmaceutical Care Practice* (New York: McGraw-Hill, 1998).

Chapter 5

1. Beverly Daniel Tatum, *Can We Talk about Race? And Other Conversations in an Era of School Resegregation* (New York: Basic Books, 2007).

2. For a clear and concise explanation of the phases of White and Black racial identity formation, I suggest Beverly Daniel Tatum's *Why Are All the Black Kids Sitting Together in the Cafeteria?*

3. Lilia I. Bartholome and Donald P. Macedo, "Dancing with Bigotry: The Poisoning of Racial and Ethnic Identities," in *Critical Ethnicity: Countering the Waves of Identity Politics*, ed. Robert H. Tai and Mary L. Kenyatta (Lanham, Md.: Rowman and Littlefield, 1999): 65–91.

4. See appendix B for suggested readings.

5. Myles Horton and Paulo Freire, *We Make the Road by Walking: Conversations on Education and Social Change*, ed. Brenda Bell and John Gaventa (Philadelphia: Temple University Press, 1991).

Chapter 6

1. Shelley H. Billig, *Unpacking What Works in Service-Learning: Promising Research-Based Practices to Improve Student Outcomes*, Growing to Greatness (Minneapolis: NYLC, 2007).

2. Billig, *Unpacking What Works in Service-Learning*.

3. Billig, *Unpacking What Works in Service-Learning*.

4. Harvey F. Silver, Richard W. Strong, and Matthew J. Perini, *The Strategic Teacher: Selecting the Right Research-Based Strategy for Every Lesson* (Upper Saddle River, N.J.: Pearson Education, 2009). Silver, Strong, and Perini describe four types of questions in *The Strategic Teacher*. From figure 1.4, Questions in Style, p. 31.

5. Susan Cipolle and Lisa Lenhart-Murphy, "Making It Work: Connecting Service to the Curriculum" (paper presented at the National Service-Learning Conference, Minneapolis, April 2003).

6. Billig, *Unpacking What Works in Service-Learning.*

7. Billig, *Unpacking What Works in Service-Learning.*

8. Billig, *Unpacking What Works in Service-Learning.*

9. Billig, *Unpacking What Works in Service-Learning.*

10. Billig, *Unpacking What Works in Service-Learning.*

11. Billig, *Unpacking What Works in Service-Learning.*

12. Dwight E. Giles, Jr., and Janet Elyer, "The Theoretical Roots of Service-Learning in John Dewey: Toward a Theory of Service-Learning," *Michigan Journal of Community Service Learning* 1, no. 1 (1994): 77–85.

13. Timothy K. Stanton, Dwight E. Giles, and Nadinne I. Cruz, *Service-Learning: A Movement's Pioneers Reflect on Its Origins, Practice, and Future* (San Francisco: Jossey-Bass, 1999).

14. Robert L. Sigmon, "Service-Learning: Three Principles," *Synergis*, 1979, 9, 10. Quoted/cited in Stranton, Giles, and Cruz, *Service Learning.*

15. Stanton, Giles, and Cruz, *Service-Learning.*

16. RMC Research (www.rmcresearchcorporation.com) is a national leader in program research and evaluation, professional development, consultation, and product development.

17. NYLC (www.nylc.org), founded in 1982, is committed to linking "youth, educators and communities to redefine the role of young people in society." The vehicle for empowerment is service-learning, through which students become valuable sources of information and resources as they contribute to the community. Each year NYLC conducts trainings for students and teachers, hosts the National Service-Learning Conference, and supports research and project implementation.

18. The K–12 Service Learning Standards for Quality Practice are available for download at the NYLC website (www.nylc.org/standards) and were published in Growing to Greatness in 2008. Permission to reprint granted June 2009.

Chapter 7

1. Paulo Freire, quoted in James W. Fraser, "Love and History in the Work of Paulo Freire," in *Mentoring the Mentor: A Critical Dialogue with Paulo Freire*, by Paulo Freire (New York: Peter Lang, 1997): 175–199.

2. Paulo Freire, *Pedagogy of the Oppressed*, trans. M. B. Ramos (1970; repr., New York: Continuum, 1993).

3. Ira Shor, *Empowering Education: Critical Teaching for Social Change* (Chicago: University of Chicago Press, 1992).

4. Ira Shor, referenced in Susan Cipolle, "Service-Learning as a Counterhegemonic Practice: Evidence Pro and Con," *Multicultural Education* 11, no. 3 (2004): 12–23.

5. Shor, *Empowering Education*.

6. Stephen D. Brookfield, *Becoming a Critically Reflective Teacher* (San Francisco: Jossey-Bass, 1995).

7. Brookfield, *Becoming a Critically Reflective Teacher*.

8. Freire, *Pedagogy of the Oppressed*.

9. Gloria Ladson-Billings, "Yes, But How Do We Do It?" in *White Teachers/ Diverse Classrooms: A Guide to Building Inclusive Schools, Promoting High Expectations, and Eliminating Racism*, ed. Julie Landsman and Chance W. Lewis (Sterling, Va.: Stylus, 2006), 29–42.

10. Bill Bigelow, "Testing, Tracking and Toeing the Line," in *Rethinking Our Classrooms: Teaching for Equity and Justice*, ed. Bill Bigelow (Milwaukee: Rethinking Schools, 1994): 117–24.

11. Shor, *Empowering Education*.

12. Freire, *Pedagogy of the Oppressed*.

13. Thomas Groome, *Educating for Life: A Spiritual Vision for Every Teacher and Parent* (New York: Crossroad Publishing, 1998).

14. Joe Kincheloe and Shirley R. Steinberg, *Changing Multiculturalism: New Times, New Curriculum* (Bristol, Pa.: Open University Press, 1997); and Pepi Leistyna, *Defining and Designing Multiculturalism: One School System's Efforts* (New York: State University of New York Press, 2002).

15. The *Frankfurt school* is a term that denotes the thinkers in the Institute for Social Research at the University of Frankfurt am Main in Germany in the 1930s. These thinkers focused on radical social change, using the term "critical theory of society" to describe their work, based in the work of Karl Marx and Immanuel Kant's critical philosophy. They were working to create revolutionary agency in society, comparing sociological ideology with sociological reality in terms of human freedom and happiness.

16. *Liberation theology* is a Christian school of theology, particularly Roman Catholic in nature, emphasizing the mission of social justice for the poor and oppressed through political activism.

Chapter 8

1. Quote from Vito Perrone, Director of Teacher Education, Harvard Graduate school of Education at the 1992 Council of Chief State School Officers' Service-learning Conference in Racine Wisconsin

2. Benilde–St. Margaret's School, "Program of Studies," at www.bsm-online.org (accessed July 23, 2008).

3. Informed by Susan Cipolle and Lisa Lenhart-Murphy, "What Now? What Next: Sustaining Service Learning" (paper presented at the National Service-Learning Conference, Denver, April 2001).

4. Sharon Daloz Parks, *Big Questions, Worthy Dreams: Mentoring Young Adults in Their Search for Meaning, Purpose, and Faith* (San Francisco: Jossey-Bass, 2000).

5. Anne Colby and others, eds., *Educating Citizens: Preparing America's Undergraduates for Lives of Moral and Civic Responsibility* (San Francisco: Jossey-Bass, 2003).

6. Richard Kiely, "A Chameleon with a Complex: Searching for Transformation in International Service-Learning," *Michigan Journal of Community Service Learning* 10, no. 2 (2004): 5–20; and Richard Kiely, "A Transformative Learning Model for Service-Learning: A Longitudinal Case Study," *Michigan Journal of Community Service Learning* 12, no. 1 (2005): 5–22.

Chapter 9

1. Informed by Zach Zeckser, faith-formation teacher, and Lisa Lenhart-Murphy, service-learning coordinator, at Benilde–St. Margaret's School, St. Louis Park, Minn.

2. Feed My Starving Children, "About Us," at www.fmsc.org/Page.aspx?pid=264; and "Our Food," at www.fmsc.org/Page.aspx?pid=230 (accessed July 20, 2009).

3. Robert K. Greenleaf, *The Servant as Leader* (Westfield, Ind.: Greenleaf Center, 1970). For more information, visit the Greenleaf Center for Servant Leadership at www.greenleaf.org.

4. Kent Keith, "The Case for Servant Leadership" (paper presented at the Public Forum for Servant Leadership, University of St. Thomas, St. Paul, Minn., April 2009).

5. Greenleaf, *The Servant as Leader*.

6. Zach Zeckser, "Servant Leadership: Helping BSM to Realize Its Vision" (paper presented at Benilde–St. Margaret's School In-Service, St. Louis Park, Minn., October 2009).

7. Benilde–St. Margaret's School, at www.bsm-online.org (accessed September 21, 2009).

8. Ashoka, "What Is a Social Entrepreneur?" at www.ashoka.org/social_entrepreneur, and "Mission," at www.ashoka.org/visionmission (accessed June 29, 2009).

9. Skoll Foundation, "About the Skoll Foundation," at www.skollfoundation .org/ aboutskoll/index.asp, and "What Is a Social Entrepreneur?" at www.skollfoundation.org/aboutsocialentrepreneurship/whatis.asp (accessed June 29, 2009).

10. Participant Media, "Our Mission," at www.participantmedia.com/company/about_us.php, and "Our History," at www.participantmedia.com/company/history .php (accessed June 29, 2009).

11. "Facts and Statistics" at www.kiva.org/about/facts/ (accessed November 25, 2009).

12. Kiva, "What Is Kiva?" at www.kiva.org/about, "Supporters," at www.kiva.org/ about/supporters/, and "Facts and Statistics," at www.kiva.org/about/facts/ (accessed September 21, 2009).

13. Lisa Lenhart-Murphy, "Service-Learning: It's Not More Work, It's Just Different Work" (PowerPoint presented at Benilde–St. Margaret's School In-Service Learning Workshop, St. Louis Park, Minn., February 2009).

14. Lisa Lenhart-Murphy, "Service-Learning: It's Not More Work, It's Just Different Work."

Glossary

1. Samuel P. Oliner and Peral M. Oliner, *The Altruistic Personality: Rescuers of Jews in Nazi Europe* (New York: Free Press, 1990) cited in Daloz, *Common Fire.*

2. Brookfield, *The Power of Critical Theory: Liberating Adult Learning and Teaching* (San Francisco: Jossey-Bass, 2005).

3. Daloz and others, *Common Fire*, 69.

4. Peter McLaren, *Life in Schools: An Introduction to Critical Pedagogy in the Foundations of Education* (New York: Longman, 1998), 185.

5. Anne Colby and others, eds., *Educating Citizens: Preparing America's Undergraduates for Lives of Moral and Civic Responsibility* (San Francisco: Jossey-Bass, 2003), 65.

Bibliography

Ashoka International. "Vision and Mission." www.ashoka.org/visionmission (accessed August 17, 2009).

———. "What Is a Social Entrepreneur?" www.ashoka.org/social_entrepreneur (accessed August 17, 2009).

Astin, Alexander W., Linda J. Sax, and Juan Avalos. "Long-Term Effects of Volunteerism during the Undergraduate Years." *The Review of Higher Education* 22 (1999): 187–202.

Banks, James A., and Cherry A. McGee Banks. *Multicultural Education: Issues and Perspectives*. 3rd ed. Hoboken, N.J.: Wiley, 1997.

Battistani, Richard M. "The Service Learner as Engaged Citizen." *Metropolitan Universities: An International Forum* 7, no. 1 (Summer 1996): 85–98.

Benilde–St. Margaret's. "Program of Studies." www.bsm-online.org/courses.aspx (accessed August 17, 2009).

Bigelow, Bill., ed. *Rethinking Our Classrooms: Teaching for Equity and Justice*. Milwaukee: Rethinking Schools, 1994.

Billig, Shelley H. "Research on K–12 School-Based Service-Learning: The Evidence Builds." *Phi Delta Kappan* 81 (2000): 658–64, http://www.pdkmembers.org/members_online/members/orders.asp?action=results&t=A&desc=Research+on+K-12+school-based+service-learning&text=&lname_1=billig&fname_1=&lname_2=&fname_2=&kw_1=&kw_2=&kw_3=&kw_4=&mn1=5&yr1=2000&mn2=&yr2=&c1= (accessed November 25, 2009).

———. "Unpacking What Works in Service-Learning: Promising Research-Based Practices to Improve Student Outcomes." Growing to Greatness. Minneapolis: NYLC, 2007.

Boyle-Baise, Marilynne. "Community Service-Learning for Multicultural Education: An Exploratory Study with Preservice Teachers." *Equity and Excellence* 32 (1998): 52–60.

———. *Multicultural Service Learning: Educating Teachers in Diverse Communities.* New York: Teachers College Press, 2002.

Boyle-Baise, Marilynne, and James Langford. "There Are Children Here: Service-Learning for Social Justice." *Equity and Excellence* 37 (2004): 55–66.

Boyle-Baise, Marilynne, and Christine E. Sleeter. "Community-Based Service Learning for Multicultural Teacher Education." *Educational Foundations* 14, no. 2 (2000): 33–50.

Brookfield, Stephen. D. *Becoming a Critically Reflective Teacher.* San Francisco: Jossey-Bass, 1995.

———. *The Power of Critical Theory: Liberating Adult Learning and Teaching.* San Francisco: Jossey-Bass, 2005.

Carolyn O'Grady, ed. *Integrating Service Leaning and Multicultural Education in Colleges and Universities.* Mahwah, N.J.: Erlbaum, 2000.

Cipolle, Robert J., Linda M. Strand, and Peter C. Morley. *Pharmaceutical Care Practice.* New York: McGraw-Hill, 1998.

Cipolle, Susan. "Service-Learning and Social Justice: Effects of Early Experiences." PhD diss., University of St. Thomas, 2006.

———. "Service-Learning as a Counter-Hegemonic Practice: Evidence Pro and Con." *Multicultural Education* 11, no. 3 (2004): 12–23.

Cipolle, Susan, and Lisa Lenhart. "What Now? What Next? Sustaining Service Learning." Paper presented at the National Service-Learning Conference, Denver, April 2001.

Cipolle, Susan, and Lisa Lenhart-Murphy. "Making It Work: Connecting Service to the Curriculum." Paper presented at the National Service-Learning Conference, Minneapolis, April 2003.

Claus, Jeff, and Curtis Ogden, eds. *Service Learning for Youth Empowerment and Social Change.* New York: Peter Lang, 1999.

Colby, Anne, Thomas Ehrlich, Elizabeth Beaumont, and Jason Stephens, eds. *Educating Citizens: Preparing America's Undergraduates for Lives of Moral and Civic Responsibility.* San Francisco: Jossey-Bass, 2003.

Cooks, Leda, Erica Scharrer, and Mari Castaneda Paredes. "Toward a Social Approach to Learning in Community Service Learning." *Michigan Journal of Community Service Learning* 10, no. 2 (2004): 44–56.

Daloz, Laurent A. Parks, Cheryl Keen, James P. Keen, and Sharon Daloz Parks. *Common Fire: Leading Lives of Commitment in a Complex World.* Boston: Beacon Press, 1996.

Erikson, Erik H. *Identity: Youth and Crisis.* New York: Norton, 1968.

Eyler, Janet, and Dwight E. Giles, Jr. *Where's the Learning in Service-Learning?* San Francisco: Jossey-Bass, 1999.

Feed My Starving Children. "About Us." www.fmsc.org/Page.aspx?pid=264 (accessed August 17, 2009).

———. "Our Food." www.fmsc.org/Page.aspx?pid=230 (accessed August 17, 2009).

Freire, Paulo. *Education for Critical Consciousness.* Translated by M. B. Ramos. 1973. New York: Continuum, 2002.

———. *Mentoring the Mentor: A Critical Dialogue with Paulo Freire.* Counterpoints: Studies in the Postmodern Theory of Education 60. New York: Peter Lang, 1997.

———. *Pedagogy of the Oppressed.* Translated by M. B. Ramos. 1970. New York: Continuum, 1993.

Giles, Dwight E., Jr., and Janet Elyer. "The Theoretical Roots of Service-Learning in John Dewey: Toward a Theory of Service-Learning." *Michigan Journal of Community Service Learning* 1, no. 1 (1994): 77–85.

Gilligan, Carol. *In a Different Voice: Psychological Theory and Women's Development.* Cambridge, Mass.: Harvard University Press, 1982.

Giroux, Henry A. *Teachers as Intellectuals: Toward a Critical Pedagogy of Learning.* Westport, Conn.: Bergin and Garvey, 1988.

Giroux, Henry A., and Peter L. McLaren, eds. *Critical Pedagogy, the State and Cultural Struggle.* Albany: State University of New York Press, 1989.

Greenleaf, Robert K. *The Servant as Leader.* Westfield, Ind.: Greenleaf Center, 1970.

Groome, Thomas. *Educating for Life: A Spiritual Vision for Every Teacher and Parent.* New York: Crossroad Publishing, 1998.

hooks, bell. *Teaching to Transgress: Education as the Practice of Freedom.* New York: Routledge, 1994.

hooks, bell, and Cornel West. *Breaking Bread: Insurgent Black Intellectual Life.* Toronto: Between the Lines, 1991.

Horton, Myles, and Paulo Freire. *We Make the Road by Walking: Conversations on Education and Social Change,* edited by Brenda Bell and John Gaventa. Philadelphia: Temple University Press, 1991.

Kahne, Joseph, Joel Westheimer, and Bethany Rogers. "Service-Learning and Citizenship: Directions for Research." Special issue, *Michigan Journal of Community Service Learning* 7 (2000): 42–51.

———. *In the Service of What? The Politics of Service Learning.* In J. Claus & C. Ogden (Eds.), *Service Learning for Youth Empowerment and Social Change.* New York: Peter Lang. Pp 25–42, http://infortrac.gale.groupe.com/itw/informark/147/559/28754730w2/purl=re1_AEIM_0_A18434556&dyn=8!xrn_1_0_a18434556?sw_acp=clic_stthomas (accessed October 17, 2002), 1999.

Keith, Kent. *The Case for Servant Leadership.* Paper presented at University of St. Thomas Public Forum for Servant Leadership, St. Paul, Minn., April, 2009.

Kiely, Richard. "A Chameleon with a Complex: Searching for Transformation in International Service-Learning." *Michigan Journal of Community Service Learning* 10, no. 2 (2004): 5–20.

———. "A Transformative Learning Model for Service-Learning: A Longitudinal Case Study." *Michigan Journal of Community Service Learning* 12, no. 1 (2005): 5–22.

Kincheloe, Joe, and Shirley R. Steinberg. *Changing Multiculturalism: New Times, New Curriculum.* Bristol, Pa.: Open University Press, 1997.

Kiva. "Press Center: Facts and Statistics." www.kiva.org/about/facts/ (accessed August 17, 2009).

——. "Supporters." www.kiva.org/about/supporters (accessed August 17, 2009).

——. "What Is Kiva?" www.kiva.org/about (accessed August 17, 2009).

Koliba, Christopher J. "Service-Learning and Downsizing of Democracy: Learning Our Way Out." *Michigan Journal of Community Service Learning* 10, no. 2 (2004), 57–68.

Landsman, Julie, and Chance W. Lewis, eds. *White Teachers/Diverse Classrooms: A Guide to Building Inclusive Schools, Promoting High Expectations, and Eliminating Racism.* Sterling, Va.: Stylus, 2006.

Leistyna, Pepi. *Defining and Designing Multiculturalism: One School System's Efforts.* New York: State University of New York Press, 2002.

Lenhart-Murphy, Lisa. "Service-Learning: It's Not More Work, It's Just Different Work." Paper presented at Benilde–St. Margaret's Service-Learning Workshop, St. Louis Park, Minn., February 2009.

Maybach, Carol Wiechman. "Investigating Urban Community Needs: Service Learning from a Social Justice Perspective." *Education and Urban Society* 28 (1996): 224–36.

McLaren, Peter. *Life in Schools: An Introduction to Critical Pedagogy in the Foundations of Education.* New York: Longman, 1998.

Merriam-Webster Online Dictionary. http://www.merriam-webster.com/dictionary/charity.

Metz, Edward, Jeffrey McLellan, and James Youniss. "Types of Voluntary Service and Adolescents' Civic Development." *Journal of Adolescent Research* 18 (2003): 188–203.

Mezirow, Jack, ed. *Learning as Transformation: Critical Perspectives on a Theory in Progress.* San Francisco: Jossey-Bass, 2000.

Moore, Kim Patrick, and Judith Haymore Sandholtz. "Designing Successful Service Learning Projects for Urban Schools." *Urban Education* 34, no. 4 (1999): 480–98.

Morton, Keith, and John Saltmarsh. "Addams, Day, and Dewey: The Emergence of Community Service in American Culture." *Michigan Journal of Community Service Learning* 4 (Fall 1997): 137–49.

National Youth Leadership Council. "K–12 Service Learning Standards for Quality Practice." www.nylc.org/standards (accessed August 17, 2009).

——. "What Is Service Learning?" nylc.org/wisl/index.html (accessed August 17, 2009).

Nieto, Sonia. *Affirming Diversity: The Sociopolitical Context of Multicultural Education.* New York: Addison Wesley Longman, 2000.

Noddings, Nel. *Caring: A Feminine Approach to Ethics and Moral Education.* Berkeley: University of California Press, 1984.

Parks, Sharon Daloz. *Big Questions, Worthy Dreams: Mentoring Young Adults in Their Search for Meaning, Purpose, and Faith.* San Francisco: Jossey-Bass, 2000.

Rhoads, Robert A. *Community Service and Higher Learning: Explorations of the Caring Self*. Albany: State University of New York Press, 1997.

Rhoads, Robert A., and Jeffrey P.F. Howard, eds. *Academic Service Learning: A Pedagogy of Action and Reflections*. San Francisco: Jossey-Bass, 1998.

RMC Research Corporation. www.rmcresearchcorporation.com (accessed August 17, 2009).

Robinson, Tony. "Dare the School Build a New Social Order?" *Michigan Journal of Community Service Learning* 7 (Fall 2000): 142–57.

Saltmarsh, John. "Education for Critical Citizenship: John Dewey's Contribution to the Pedagogy of Community Service-Learning." *Michigan Journal of Community Service Learning* 3 (Fall 1996): 13–21.

Shor, Ira. *Empowering Education: Critical Teaching for Social Change*. Chicago: University of Chicago Press, 1992.

Silver, Harvey F., Richard W. Strong, and Matthew J. Perini. *The Strategic Teacher: Selecting the Right Research-Based Strategy for Every Lesson*. Upper Saddle River, N.J.: Pearson Education, 2009.

Skoll Foundation. "About the Skoll Foundation." www.skollfoundation.org/about skoll/index.asp (accessed August 17, 2009).

———. "What Is a Social Entrepreneur?" www.skollfoundation.org/aboutsocialentrepreneurship/whatis.asp (accessed August 17, 2009).

Sleeter, Christine E. *Multicultural Education as Social Activism*. Albany: State University of New York Press, 1996.

Stanton, Timothy K., Dwight E. Giles, and Nadinne I. Cruz. *Service-Learning: A Movement's Pioneers Reflect on Its Origins, Practice, and Future*. San Francisco: Jossey-Bass, 1999.

Stoeker, Randy. "Community-Based Research: From Practice to Theory and Back Again." *Michigan Journal of Community Service Learning* 9, no. 2 (2003): 35–46.

Suls, Jerry, ed. *Psychological Perspectives on the Self*. Vol. 4, *The Self in Social Perspective*. Hillsdale, N.J.: Erlbaum, 1993.

Tatum, Beverly Daniel. *Can We Talk about Race? And Other Conversations in an Era of School Resegregation*. New York: Basic Books, 2007.

———. *Why Are All the Black Kids Sitting Together in the Cafeteria? And Other Conversations about Race*. New York: Basic Books, 1997.

Verba, S., Scholzman, K. L. & Brady, H. E. *Voice and Equality: Civic Volunteerism in American Politics*. Cambridge, MA: Harvard University Press, 1995.

Vogelgesang, Lori J., and Alexander W. Astin. "Comparing the Effects of Community Service and Service Learning." *Michigan Journal of Community Service Learning* 7, no. 1 (2000): 25–34.

Wade, Rahima C. "Social Action in the Social Studies: From the Ideal to the Real." *Theory into Practice* 40, no. 1 (2001): 23–28.

Warneken, Felix, and Michael Tomasello. "Altruistic Helping in Human Infants and Young Chimpanzees." *Science* 311, no. 5765 (3 March 2006): 1301–3.

Warren, Karen. "Educating Students for Social Justice in Service Learning." *Journal of Experiential Education* 21, no. 3 (1998): 134–39.

Weah, Wokie, Verna Cornelia Simmons, and McClellan Hall. "Service-Learning and Multicultural/Multiethnic Perspectives: From Diversity to Equity." *Phi Delta Kappan* 81, no. 9 (2000): 673–75.

Yates, Miranda, and James Youniss., eds. *Roots of Civic Identity: International Perspectives on Community Service and Activism in Youth.* Cambridge: Cambridge University Press, 2003.

Youniss, J., & Yates, M. *Community Service and Social Responsibility in Youth.* Chicago: University of Chicago Press, 1997.

Zeckser, Zach. "Servant Leadership: Helping BSM to Realize Its Vision." Paper presented at Benilde–St. Margaret's School In-Service, St. Louis Park, Minn., October 2009.

About the Author

Susan Benigni Cipolle is assistant to the president, World Language Department chair, and a French teacher at Benilde–St. Margaret's School in St. Louis Park, Minnesota. In addition, the author is an adjunct faculty member in the College of Applied Professional Studies graduate program in curriculum and instruction at University of St. Thomas, where she teaches courses in diversity and multicultural education.

Her educational experience spans four decades, and as an administrator and service-learning practitioner, she was instrumental in developing and institutionalizing the service-learning program at Benilde–St. Margaret's School. In addition, Dr. Cipolle's responsibilities include strategic planning and grant solicitation and implementation. The author has presented several papers on service-learning and social justice at state and national conferences.

Dr. Cipolle received a BA in French from Northern Illinois University, an MS in learning technologies, and an EdD in critical pedagogy from the University of St. Thomas in St. Paul, Minnesota. Honors received include BSM Faculty of the Year, an American Association of Teachers of French *Stage Pédagogique* scholarship, and an American Council on the Teaching of Foreign Languages Laval University scholarship.